JUDITH COHEN

THE SIX ANONYMOUS L'HOMME ARMÉ MASSES

MUSICOLOGICAL STUDIES AND DOCUMENTS

ARMEN CARAPETYAN, Ph. D.
General Editor

THE SIX ANONYMOUS *L'HOMME ARMÉ* MASSES

IN

NAPLES, BIBLIOTECA NAZIONALE, MS VI E 40

by

JUDITH COHEN

MUSICOLOGICAL STUDIES AND DOCUMENTS

21

JUDITH COHEN

THE SIX ANONYMOUS L'HOMME ARMÉ MASSES

IN

NAPLES, BIBLIOTECA NAZIONALE, MS VI E 40

AMERICAN INSTITUTE OF MUSICOLOGY

1968

CONTENTS

ACKNOWLEDGEMENTS

The present study originated as a Ph. D. dissertation at the University of Zurich, under the supervision of Prof. Dr. Kurt von Fischer. It is my pleasant duty to express my sincerest thanks to Prof. von Fischer, who introduced me into the secrets of methodical and down-to-earth research, basis for any comprehensive understanding of contexts and relations.

I also wish to thank the following persons and institutions: the Biblioteca Nazionale, Naples, kindly gave me access to the manuscript studied, and its librarians helped me with bibliographical advice; the Biblioteca Marciana, Venice, and the Bibliothèque Royale de Belgique, Brussels, gave me considerable assistance in clarifying problems of heraldry and paleography. Valuable aid in heraldic researches was also offered to me by Prof. Dr. Dénes Bartha, Budapest, Dr. Florens Deuchler, Bonn, and M. Meurgey de Tupigny, Paris. Prof. Dr. Hans Haefele, Munich, kindly helped me in questions of medieval Latin linguistics, Dr. Peter Meller, Florence, gave me important historical references concerning the relations between Buda, Naples and Burgundy in the late fifteenth century, and Mrs. Lydia Klausner, Jerusalem, took pains with the editing in English of my paper.

To all these and to many others who supported me with advice, ideas and information, I wish to convey my heartiest thanks.

Jerusalem 1968

J. C.

FOREWORD

The folio manuscript VI E 40 of the *Biblioteca Nazionale*, Naples, was discovered by Dragan Plamenac [1]. It contains a cycle of six connected Masses on the *cantus firmus* (c.f.) *L'Homme armé* [2]. Notation and style of composition point to the second half of the 15th century and the Franco-Flemish circle [3].

The enormous popularity of the *L'Homme armé* melody in the 15th and 16th centuries is evident from its frequent use by the leading composers of this epoch. The tune appears as c.f. in more than 30 Masses from Dufay to Carissimi, and many chansons, double chansons, quodlibets and even instrumental dances are based on this melody [4]. Plamenac's discovery of the Neapolitan Codex was of great importance, because it was thus that the text of the famous chanson first became known. This emerged from

an unusual method of writing, whereby the tenor was invariably noted down twice: once as a quotation from the original chanson, with the French secular text set to the music precisely, syllable by syllable; and once as the tenor part constituting the c.f. of the Mass section, with its corresponding liturgical textual incipit. Thus it was possible to reconstruct at least the first stanza of the chanson *L'Homme armé* [5]. (See ex. 1, p. 9).

The importance of the MS from a musical point of view lies in the fact that it contains a Mass cycle of great dimensions. The six Masses do not stand apart but are combined into a cycle by a comprehensive plan. The original *L'Homme armé* melody is divided into five sections, each forming the basis for the c.f. of one whole Mass. A canon code in Latin

1 D. Plamenac, "La chanson de *L'Homme armé* et le manuscrit VI E 40 de la Bibliothèque nationale de Naples", *Annales de la Fédération archéologique et historique de Belgique, Congrés jubilaire* (1925), 229 ff.

2 The four first Masses of the cycle have appeared in *MPLSER*, series I, vol. iii: no. 1, 2, Rome 1957, no. 3, 4, Rome 1965 (ed. by L. Feininger).

3 Cf. D. Plamenac, *op. cit.*; D. Gombosi, "Vita musicale alla Corte de Re Mattia", Corvina XII (1929), 128; G. Reese, *Music in the Renaissance*, New York 1954, 149-50.

4 See the list of L'Homme armé compositions at the appendix.

Ex. 1

hexameters prescribes the manner in which these short components should be expanded to form the c.f. of full Mass movements, and a *resolutio* states the final form of the c.f. for each section of the Mass. When the chanson has been exhaustively exploited in the first five Masses the separate sections are combined: Mass 6, closing and crowning the whole cycle, uses the complete *L'Homme armé* melody as its c.f., adding a fifth part to the four existing ones — a canonic imitation of the c.f. a fifth below the tenor.

We are, therefore, confronted with a skilfully planned structure, a unique example in the history of polyphonic ordinary Mass. It is intended here to examine these compositions individually and in relation to the whole and to arrive at an approximation of their date of origin on the basis of stylistic features, historical events and the evidence inherent in the MS itself.

[5] The *longa* rests, which appear in part A before a and b, in part B before d and e and in part A¹ again before a and b, have been omitted here.

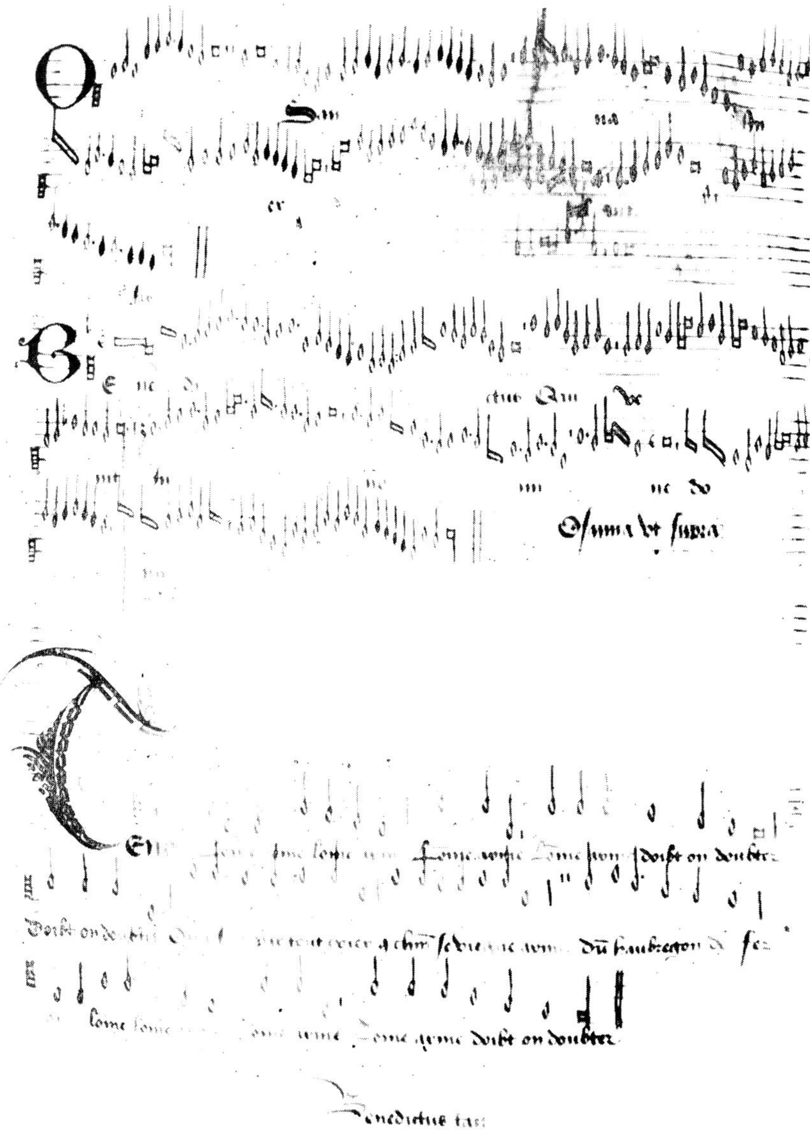

Fol. 62v. *Osanna,* Mass VI, ST

Fol. 64. Blazon

A. THE MANUSCRIPT AND ITS CONTENTS

The MS VI E 40 of the BN, Naples, is a large parchment codex in folio size (44.5 cm x 31.5 cm), consisting of 64 leaves foliotated in modern pencil on the right hand recto and on the left hand verso. The MS consists of 10 quires of 7, 7, 7, 6, 6, 8, 6, 7, 8 and 2 leaves, and has a brown leather binding, probably of the 17th century. Inside the cover is the stamp of the library and the book signature.

Folio 64 of the MS bears the Latin dedication: *Ad serenissimam Ungarie Reginam,* the first line of which reads: *Regia progenies et regi nupta beatrix.* It may be assumed that *Ungarie Regina* refers to Beatrix of Aragon (1475-1508), the wife of Matthias Corvinus [6]. Below the dedication there is a blazon, the details of which are almost indiscernible, and which bears the motto: *Que par Dieu soit.* The surface of this blazon is pale and dark blue, apparently without figures. On the upper lefthand side there is a halfmoon in an orange-red colour and inclined upwards. Blazon and motto have not been identified. Research in the Libraries of Naples (Biblioteca Nazionale), Venice (Bibl. Marciana), Budapest (University Library) and Brussels (Bibl. Royale) remained fruitless.

The front paper fly leaf of the MS is blank, while the one of the back contains a 17th-century inscription in ink: *Carlo di Francia primo di questo nome Re di Napoli e di Sicilia era figlio del Re Luigi VIII sopranimato il Lione e fratello di S. Luigi. Questo nacque nel mese di Marzo 1220 e sposo Beatrice ereditiera e quarta figlia di Raimondo Berenger Conte di Provenza. A questa Regina fu il presente manoscritto dedicato. Il titolo Ad serenissinam Ungariae Reginam è stato scritto dopo, prendendosi una svista, mentre Maria moglie di Carlo II fu Regina d'Ungheria, a quale stato poi successe Carlo Martello loro figlio.*

This inscription attempts to date the MS exclusively by the catch word "Beatrix" but fails, owing to lack of acquaintance with the musical style of the period. The existence of a Hungarian queen of Neapolitan origin was overlooked. Furthermore, *Carlo di Francia* or Charles I of Anjou (King of Naples from 1282) was born in 1226 and Charles Martel, son of Char-

6 For further details cf. p. 63 ff.

les II of Anjou (and grandson of Charles I) had died in the year 1296 without succeeding to the Hungarian throne (which, in fact, passed to his son, King Charles I of Hungary in 1309) [7].

The parchment leaves of the MS contain twelve staves of five lines each. The music is noted down in large figures in red and black ink, by the same hand throughout. In all but two places the graphic layout of the MS is strictly adhered to. *Superius* and tenor on the *verso*, alto and bass (*contratenores* as they are called throughout) on the *recto* side. The two exceptions are fol. 13v and 16v which contain all the four parts, while the following fol. 14r and 17r remain blank.

Examination of the MS shows that the first and last sections of all the six Masses are invariably incomplete: in the *Kyrie* the *superius* and the tenor parts are missing, whereas in the last *Agnus* it is the two *contratenores* that are absent. This means, in fact, that: 1) there is a leaf missing between two consecutive Masses, which originally bore the *superius* and the tenor of the *Kyrie* on its *verso* and the *contratenores* of the *Agnus* on the *recto*; 2) in addition, the first leaf of Mass 1 and the last leaf of Mass 6, which presumably bore the *superius* and the tenor of the *Kyrie* and the *contratenores* of the *Agnus*, are both missing. The consistent absence of the connecting leaves and of the first leaf of the first Mass may perhaps be explained by the assumption that the *superius* and the tenor parts of the first *Kyrie* movements were possibly illuminated with artistic majuscules and were therefore removed later on. Though there is no evidence of this procedure anywhere in the MS, its large size and the solemn dedication suggest that the MS may have been a richly ornamented one.

If these uniformly missing sections of the outer movements are disregarded, only Masses 3 and 5 in fact remain incomplete, while in the Masses 1, 2, 4 and 6 no further parts are missing.

In Mass 3 two leaves are missing:

1) Between fol. 27 and 28, containing:

r. :	(a)	Bass *Et incarnatus*	supplementary to fol. 27v
	(b)	Alto, bass *Resurrexit*	
v. :	(a)	*Superius*, tenor *qui ex Patre*	supplementary to fol. 28r
	(b)	,, ,, *Et expecto*	

[7] Cf. *Enciclopedia Italiana* IX, 51-52; 74-76.

2) Between fol. 29 and 30, containing:

r. :	(a)	Alto, bass *Pleni*	supplementary to fol. 29v
	(b)	,, ,, *Osanna* I	
v. :	(a)	*Superius Benedictus*	supplementary to fol. 30r
	(b)	,, *Osanna*	

In Mass 5 one leaf is missing between fol. 45 and 46, containing:

r. :		Alto, bass *Et in terra*	suppl. to fol. 46r
v. :	(a)	*Superius*, tenor *Qui tollis*	
	(b)	,, ,, *Cum Sancto Spiritu*	

To sum up: there are ten leaves missing altogether in the MS: seven in the outer movements of the six Masses and another three in Masses 3 and 5. The original MS appears, therefore, to have consisted of 74 folios.

Analogous to its musical contents the external form of the MS, too, follows a "graphical overall plan", which adheres to a certain order of colours. The initials of the *superius* (*i.e.* the first letter of the text concerned) and those of the *contratenores* (*i.e.* always the letter C) alternate between blue and red, while the letter T for the tenor alternates with similar regularity between yellow and black. This T is slightly ornamented, at times taking the form of an arabesque, at others the somewhat distorted profile of a man (8v, 12v, 23v, 39v, 43v, 50v, 60v), or (32v) the form of a fish. However, at the *resolutio* all ornamentation and even the designation "tenor" are omitted. All these features stress the special status of the chanson quotation in the Masses.

The musical notation tallies in every particular with late 15th century notation. The only special feature of the MS is the alternation between red and black ink, which has no significance of coloration but whose meaning becomes clear in the scoring of the parts: tenorless passages, sections or movements are written in red, those containing a tenor part are in black ink [8]. The change of colours occurs almost without exception in all three parts simultaneously. On the whole the rule is so rigidly observed that often a note which still belongs to a section containing a tenor part is written in black, whereas the *punctus additionis*, which extends its duration beyond the tenor's domain, is already red.

[8] In Ms Oxford Bodl. Selden B 26 (OS) the reverse of this procedure is found. There the *cantus planus* is written in red, in order to distinguish it from the other parts. Cf. article "Color", *MGG* II, 1570.

A similar method of notation (with changing colours) is extant in the MS Eton 178, whose compilation is dated by Ll. Harrison between 1490-1502 [9]. There the change of colour is confined to the text and seems to point to a solo performance of the red sections of the Antiphon and the Magnificat pieces, which were intended for a smaller number of performers and are rhythmically more intricate. The important rôle played by changes of timbre in the Eton MS is corroborated by the various combinations of high and low vocal registers so typical of the compositions in that manuscript. It may therefore be assumed that in our MS, too, change of colour is to be interpreted as change of sonority, for here too, distinction is made between sections containing c.f. and those that do not. This has misled at least one scholar into thinking that the interchange between red and black ink is intended to distinguish between sections written in 3/2 meter, which are slower and richer in thirds, and between livelier sections proceeding in hemioles [10]. This is no doubt a confusion of symptom and cause. The point of departure in these Masses is the tenor, the presence and absence of which determines the musical texture of the composition. Sections containing the tenor part are always full voiced (there are no two- or three-part passages in which the tenor participates); consequently their sonority is more euphonic and their movement somewhat halting. Tenorless passages, in contrast, are more polyphonic, rhythmically more complicated and with greater melodic differentiation. It seems obvious that these passages were intended for solo performance and that this was indicated by means of change in colour. Indeed, though the formula: c.f.-containing passages = choral, c.f.-less passages = solistic, would seem to be overschematic, yet it does reemphasize the "tenor centered" attitude so characteristic of these Masses, this time from the aspect of sonority.

The tenor part moves in longdrawn notes which are not — nor can they be — matched by any text; only the beginning of the text is indicated. It may therefore be assumed that the tenor part was intended for instrumental performance [11], an assumption which is further reinforced by the *canon* of the fourth Mass:

[9] Cf. his article "Eton, MS 178", *MGG* III, 1591 ff., as well as his "The Eton Choirbook, its Background and Contents", *Annales Musicologiques* I (1953), 151 ff.

[10] E. Mancusi Ungaro, "Il Liber Coralis notis musicis ornatus, MS VI 40", *Il Rievocatore* XII, no. 1-3 (1961).

[11] The presence of the textual incipit only indicates, according to H. Besseler, instrumental performance. Cf. *Dufay* O IV, p. III.

"Buccina clangorem voces vertendo reflectit
Subque gradu reboat iterum clamando quaterno".

It is, in fact, the trombone which plays the tenor part, and which accentuates the rôle of the tenor with its dark timbre [12]. Thus the change of colour may have served as an optical aid to the player who stood behind the singers, and may have given him his entrance lead.

Apart from the changes of colours, the notation does not differ from that practised in the late 15th century. The ligatures, too, are typical for this period. The sole exception is the antiquated form ⊒ for *brevis-longa*, which is found side by side with the usual form ᑕᑎ (in the *Qui tollis* of the second Mass, for example, both forms of the ligature are used in the bass).

As far as time is concerned, the *tempus perfectum* still dominates in these Masses, although, in deference to the principles of *varietas*, it is varied with imperfect tempi. The *prolatio maior*, on the other hand, is not used. It is interesting to note the relation between the meter of the chanson quotation and its solution. This is demonstrated below by the changes in the length of the *semibrevis*, the *integer valor* of the late 15th century:

Chanson quotation			*Resolutio*		
C·	◇	=	O	▭	(augmentation)
Ↄ·	◇	=	O	◇	(cancelation of augmentation)
C3	◇	=	Ȼ	ꟷ|	or: O ▭·

Only in Mass 4 the signatures are changed without reasonable motivation and the following relation results:

Chanson quotation			*Resolutio*	
C·	◇	=	O	◇
O	◇	=	⊙	▭
C3	◇·	=	Ȼ	▭·

[12] According to C. Sachs, *Reallexikon der Musikinstrumente*, Berlin 1913, *Buccina* meant in the Middle Ages "ein Signalhorn mässiger Grösse". On the etymology *buccine - buisine - Posaune* cf. C. Sachs, *The History of Musical Instruments*, New York 1950, 281. On the role of the trombone in the Masses of the early fifteenth century see also H. Besseler, "Die Entstehung der Posaune", *Acta* XXII (1950), 8 ff.

In Masses 2, 3 and 6 the relation between tenor and *resolutio* is indicated by the numbers 1, 2, 3, 4 and 6. The following relations are established:

Chanson	quotation	*Resolutio*		
1	𝆺	○	𝆺	
2	𝆺	○	𝆸	(or ○ 𝆹 in Mass 2)
4	𝆺	○	𝆸	
6	𝆺	₵	𝆸	

The pattern of time relation in each of these Masses is rigidly observed: in Mass 3, for example, the *semibrevis* of the chanson quotation at the sign 2 always changes in the *resolutio* into a *longa* at the sign C (2 𝆺 ≐ ₵ 𝆸), and never into a *brevis* at O, and in Mass 2 the relation 2 𝆺 = ○ 𝆹 is maintained equally strictly. This practice seems to conform to the principle of the tenor models (see below).

The time signatures of the *cantus firmi* and of the other parts almost invariably correspond, except for the sections over the c.f. in C, a signature which never occurs in the upper parts. In Mass 6 the number which precedes the chanson does not indicate the relation between quotation and resolution, but that of c.f. and upper parts, the c.f. uniformly appearing in its *integer valor* without any indication of time.

The underlaying of the text is very negligently done, as is frequently the case in the 15th century. Words are arbitrarily underlayed to music: repeat of words is not marked; words are separated by long pauses. Short passages of the text are often omitted in one part, other passages extended, whereas a more rationalized matching of text and music in each part could have avoided omissions and prolongations. The *superius* alone, owing to its more declamatory character, enjoys a more careful treatment of the text.

In Masses 3, 4 and 5 the setting of the full *Credo* text is curtailed by the simultaneous use of two passages of the text: the passage from *Et in Spiritum Sanctum* to *Confiteor* is twice set to two different texts, although the procedure differs in each case. In Mass 4 *superius* and bass bring the text up to *non erit finis*, subsequently continuing from *Et unam sanctam*, while the intermediate passage is sung by the alto parallel with the other texts. Finally all the voices join in, singing the last section of the *Credo* — *Confiteor*. However, in Mass 5 *superius* and bass sing the complete text from *Crucifixus* to *non erit finis*, while at the same time the alto leads straight on from *Et in Spiritu* to *et apostolicam ecclesiam*. In the first section of the *Credo* of Mass 3, *superius* and bass stop at *descendit de celis*, while the alto condenses the text, ending the passage on *et homo factus est*. It is interesting that the following passage is again devoted to the same text — *et incarnatus . . . homo factus est*, up to the words *sepultus est*. Unfortunately the leaf which probably bore the two *contratenor* parts (fol. 27v) is missing, so that it is impossible to determine whether the alto repeats the same passage or pauses here, since it has already sung this same text.

Summing up, it is true to say that in these Masses no single word is given special value, a tradition recalling that of the isorhythmic motet, still extant in the 15th century. Characteristic of the style of these Masses, it is always the alto which comprises the whole text in condensed form.

In several sections of the Masses short passages of text appear to be missing, yet these phrases are usually taken up by one of the other voices so that the composer ensures that the text of the Mass is set at least once in its entity.

We can, therefore, only agree in part with O. Gombosi when he writes [13]: "Devo qui recordare che per conseguenza il codice non servi mai agli scopi d'una musica pratica e meno che mai a quelli della musica liturgica, in parte perchè il testo delle messe non è completo, in parte perchè il testo musicale è tanto difettoso, che è necessaria la massima capacità inventiva per ordinarlo in partiture e completarlo".

The above description of the contents and condition of the MS proves that the Codex is not nearly so defective as was assumed by scholars hitherto, either with regard to the liturgical text or the musical text it contains. The text is intact and in the music — apart from Masses 3 and 5 — only the aforementioned parts of the external movements are missing, and even these can be reconstructed. However, if this cyclic composition is unsuitable for actual and more especially for liturgical performance — and here we must agree with Gombosi — it is due not to lack of certain details but to its towering dimensions, not to its incompleteness, as it were, but to an over abundance. It is of course possible to perform some of the Masses from the cycle separately, but the musical representation of the overall pattern which determines the structure of this work must of necessity remain an ideal.

In a way, these Masses bring to a climax an absurdity on which the whole phenomenon of the musical composition of the Mass is based. For in itself, the whole idea of combining in one musical entity the five parts

13 "Vita musicale alla Corte di Re Mattia", 150.

of the Ordinary Mass, betrays — to quote M. Bukofzer — "the weakening of purely liturgical considerations and the strengthening of essentially aesthetic concepts" [14]. To fuse together six whole cycles of the Ordinary into one gigantic integral cycle, which it would take six Sundays to perform, signifies a victory of the speculative aesthetic spirit over the conception of earlier centuries, which was confined within narrower liturgical limitations.

14 "Caput - a Liturgical Musical Study", *Studies in Medieval and Renaissance Music*, New York 1950, 218.

B. THE L'HOMME ARMÉ CHANSON AND ITS FUNCTION IN THE CYCLE

No exact facts are known about the origin of the *L'Homme armé* chanson. The earliest source known to date is an anonymous three part song in the *Mellon Chansonnier*, in which the *L'Homme armé* chanson appears in the tenor part [15]. The three parts in this version are identical with the *cantus*, alto and tenor parts of a *L'Homme armé* chanson in four parts by the Burgundian court composer Morton [16], except that in Morton's chanson the cadences are altered by the addition of the bass part. It is therefore assumed that Morton's chanson is a later version of the anonymous rendering in the *Mellon Chansonnier* and that the latter dates from the 15th century.

The *L'Homme armé* chanson in the Mellon rendering is a double chanson. Its tenor is set to a text of the *L'Homme armé* chanson which differs slightly from the text of the Neapolitan source:

> "L'ome, l'ome, l'ome armé
> L'ome armé doibt on doubter
> On a fait par tout crier
> A l'assault, a l'assault
> D'un aubregon de fer.
> L'ome, l'ome, l'ome armé.
> L'ome armé doibt on doubter."

The text of the Cantus is particularly revealing:

> "Il sera pour vous conbatu
> Le doubté turcq, Maistre Symon;
> Certainement ce sera non?
> Et de crocq de ache abatu.

[15] Cf. M. Bukofzer, "An unknown Chansonnier of the 15th Century", *MQ* XXVIII (1942), 14 ff.

[16] Ed. by J. Marix, *Les musiciens de la cour de Bourgogne au XVe siecle (1420-1467)*, Paris 1939, 96.

Son orgueil? abatu
S'il chiet en voz mains le felon.
En peu de heure l'arés batu
Au plaisir dieu, puis dira on:
Vive Symonet le breton
Que sur le turcq s'est enbatu." [17]

The mention of a *doubté turcq* links the whole text — including the *L'Homme armé* chanson — to the "Turkish peril" which still cast its shadow over Europe's political life in the latter half of the 15th century. Ruth Hannas suggests that the *L'Homme armé* chanson may have originated as a rallying song for a renewed crusade against the Turk, a plan which exercised both Philip the Good and Charles the Bold [18]. *Maistre Symon* or *Symonet le Breton* referred to here, was a friend of Dufay's, who had been active at the Burgundian court and died (in 1473) one year before him. It is thus safe to assume that the composer of the *Mellon Chansonnier* version of the *L'Homme armé* chanson belonged to the generation of Dufay and Binchois, and maintained close ties with the Burgundian court [19].

Another key to the dating of the *L'Homme armé* chanson is to be found in the problem of time signature.

Several of the *L'Homme armé* Masses of the 15th century use the song in ☾, *e.g.* those of Ockeghem, Busnois, Caron, Faugues, De Orte, Tinctoris and Vacqueras. This *prolatio* notation which requires the directive *crescit in duplo* in the other parts (so as to adjust the balance between 6/8 and 3/2) [20], was the normal method of notation for the chanson up to 1430, and disappeared at about that time [21]. It is, therefore, justifiable to assume that Masses which use this notation for the c.f., go back to a source prior to 1430. In the *Mellon* version (as in the Morton rendering),

17 Texts after R. Hannas, "Concerning Deletions in the Polyphonic Mass Credo", *JAMS* V (1952), 168.

18 *Ibid*. Cf. also p. 71 and note 107.

19 R. Hannas even suggests that Dufay himself was the composer of the song.

20 In his *Proportionale*, III, 3 (Couss. IV, 172b) Tinctoris reproaches Busnois and Ockeghem for not having made that remark in their *L'Homme armé* Masses, and praises Dufay, who has escaped the *error anglorum* in *Se la face ay pale*. By the way, Tinctoris himself, who in his *L'Homme armé* Mass uses the c.f. in *prolatio* notation, remarks, consistent with his demand, *Crescit in duplum*. Cf. also H. Besseler, *Dufay* O III, part 2, vi.

21 Cf. H. Besseler, *Bourdon und Fauxbourdon*, Leipzig 1950, 122.

the song appears in C3, which would date it later than the hypothetical original chanson in C· which occurs also in the Neapolitan Masses [22].

The popularity of the *L'Homme armé* song as a c.f. in the Masses of the 15th and 16th centuries may have been due at first to its political topicality. Later, the exact connection with the political situation seems to have been forgotten and new, often symbolical meanings were attributed to it. Thus Regis, for instance, links his *L'Homme armé* Mass with the Antiphon of the Magnificat for the feast of St. Michael, identifying the "armed man" with the guardian angel Michael [23]. Similarly in Morales' four part *L'Homme armé* Mass the illustration, the motto and the tonality all clearly refer to Charles V [24].

In addition to the evident symbolic topicality of the *L'Homme armé* chanson, considerations of tradition and "fashion" may also have actuated composers to use this song as c.f. in their Masses and thereby to give proof of their musical ingenuity. It should be emphasized that the song, due to its melodic structure, is eminently suited to form a c.f. for a composition. The short, consecutive melodic phrases, whose ambit never exceeds a fifth, lend themselves naturally to imitation. The most obvious is the motif recalling the *Passamezzo antico* (cf. example 18, p. 43). The clearly profiled character of each motif enables the melody to be split up and the separate parts thus obtained to be delivered — as in the technique of the Parody Mass — among the various voices, without sacrifycing the melodic features of the song [25]. Lastly, the song in its entity lends itself to the most diversified use in canons. Typical examples are:

[22] Pietro Aron in his *Toscanello* in *Musica* I, chap. 38, also mentions the augmentation (*cantato per maggiore*), conditioned by the combination of C· and ○, and brings the example of the *L'Homme armé* song, which according to general opinion stems from Busnois. It seems, however, that he means Busnois' *Mass*, which raises this problem, as mentioned above. Thus the erroneous opinion has arisen, that Busnois was the composer of the *L'Homme armé* chanson. This was confirmed by the "authority" of Busnois' Mass throughout the fifteenth century. Cf. O. Strunk, "The Origin of the *L'Homme armé*' Mass", *BAMS* 1936, 25 ff. For Aron's assumption cf. quotation in D. Plamenac, "Antwort zu Gombosi", *ZfMw* XI (1929), 378.

[23] G. Reese, *Music in the Renaissance*, 114. For editions of *L'Homme armé* Masses see appendix.

[24] R. Stevenson, *Spanish Cathedral Music in the Golden Age*, Berkeley 1961, 57-8.

[25] Similar reasons and others are mentioned by E. Dent, "William Byrd and the Madrigal", *Festschrift J. Wolf* 1929, 24; C. Van den Borren, *Etudes sur le XVe siècle musical*, Anvers 1941, 179.

Faugues:	Canon at the upper fifth (the alto "pre-imitating" the tenor), interval of 1-2 time units;
Basiron:	*Kyrie II* — unison canons at interval of one, two and three time units;
Regis:	Canons, slightly varied, at the lower fifth;
Mouton:	Two, three, four and seven part canons;
De la Rue:	Mass II: canon at interval of the fifth in all sections containing a c.f.;
Pipelare:	*Confiteor* — canon at the lower fifth; *Osanna* — canon at the unison, both with changing time intervals; *Agnus III* — strict imitation at the unison (indicated by a riddle canon), interval of two time units;

Diverse canons in the Masses of Vacqueras and Compère, the mensuration canons in the *Kyrie* and *Agnus III* of De la Rue's Mass I, and the *Agnus II* in Josquin's *L'Homme armé (super voces)* [26].

The question whether the *L'Homme armé* chanson was originally a monophonic folksong or whether it originated as the tenor part of a chanson, will have to remain unsolved. Its ternary structure which, though close, is not analogous with any of the *formes fixes*; its syllabic declamation, its powerful melodic line, the lively interrupted seven-syllable pattern — all these suggest the folksong, even if "A word of caution may be in order . . . against leaping to conclusions generally about alleged folk origins of fifteenth century melodies . . ." [27].

It is also difficult to determine the original version of the *L'Homme armé* song, as composers have used the melody in many different variations and modes (cf. note 53). The earliest and most salient divergencies appearing in the extant versions are the following two:

1) The omission of the descending fifth, *i.e.* motif b′ (cf. example 1), especially in the Masses of the sixteenth century. Out of the ten *L'Homme armé* Masses of the fifteenth century, which have been published in the *MPLSER*, the following set the complete chanson (including motif b′): Dufay, Busnois, Faugues, Ockeghem (except for the *Kyrie*), Basiron,

26 For details cf. L. Feininger, *Die Frühgeschichte des Kanons*, diss. Heidelberg 1937, 53-65. See also W. Apel, "Imitation Canons on L'Homme armé", *Speculum* XXV (1950), 367-73.

27 Reese, *op. cit.*, 73, Cf. also H. Brown, *Music in the French Secular Theater 1400-1550*, Cambridge, Mass. 1963, 2. — The quotation of the song by Reese, *ibid.*, ex. 18 ("The *L'Homme armé* melody, after facsimile printed in GomB, 612 — from Naples Bibl. Naz. VI E 40"), actually renders Dufays' version of the melody.

Vacqueras (again except for the *Kyrie*). The motif does not appear in the version used by Caron, Regis, de Orto and Tinctoris.

2) The second variant which occurs frequently seems to have its point of depature in Morton's chanson, and also appears in Dufay's *L'Homme armé* Mass. Here motif d 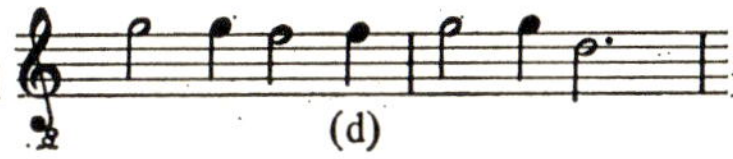

is altered upon its repetition to d′ 

. Both versions are already used by the composers of the fifteenth century. Morton and Dufay use motif d′, while Busnois and Basiron, as well as our Masses, repeat motif d twice without any variation. Some composers make use of both motifs, as does for example Ockeghem (*Kyrie, Sanctus* and *Agnus:* — d, *Gloria, Credo* — d′). Pipelare, very interestingly, uses motif d when the c.f. appears in the tenor, and the variation d′ when it appears in the bass.

The extent to which the *L'Homme armé* song is really at the centre of these Masses may be gauged from a fact previously mentioned: sometimes, side by side with the tenor part of the Mass, that portion of the original chanson quotation is noted down in the MS, which forms the basis for the c.f. of the Mass. This quotation, which preserves its French text amid the surrounding liturgical context, is singled out graphically. Its key, in the form of an illuminated T, is usually found above the *resolutio*, i.e. above the c.f. of the Mass. The secular text appears therefore to be favoured over the spiritual one.

Upon further investigation it is clear that the secular text is placed more and more at the forefront of the interest. Even the *canones* make humorous reference to the text of the chanson. It is not the c.f. melody which is to move up or down; it is the "armed man" himself. The canon of the second Mass, for instance, says:

> "Ambulat hic armatus homo, verso quoque vultu Arma rapit: dexteram sequitur, sicut vice versa ad levam scandat. Vultus sumendo priores ipse retrograditur: respondent ultima primis."

Not only the hexameter verse of the *canones*, but even the troped text of the *Kyrie* refers to the personality of the *vir armatus*. Thus the text of the *Kyrie* of the second Mass:

"Kyrie — virtutis auctor / virique creator / celli terre pontique sator — eleyson.
Kyrie — fidei miro / arma donans viro / quis cum hoste dimicet diro — eleyson.
Kyrie — cuius virtute / vir armatus tute / hostem vincit gaudet salute — eleyson.
Christe — salvator / viri potens armator / amorum dator / quibus hostis fit vir triumphator / effugatus abit temptator — eleyson.
Kyrie — spiritus alme / viro donans arma palme / dono septemplice patris nati nexus unice — eleyson."

These examples will suffice to show that to a great extent in these Masses — as indeed in the fifteenth century as a whole — the demarcation between the secular and the spiritual still remains fluid. For the *L'Homme armé* Masses discussed here, these incursions into the spiritual sphere are particularly characteristic. Graphic elaboration as well as textual evidence stress the dominating rôle of the song in these Masses. It is, however, in their musical construction that the song exercises its decisive function, as we shall see in the following chapter.

C. THE COMPOSITIONS

I. THE *CANTUS FIRMI*

1. The division of the *L'Homme armé* song

The division of the *L'Homme armé* song into five parts is made as follows:

Ex. 2

The seemingly arbitrary division of the song, espeially in sections 1-3, is surprising considering the clarity of its structure. This arbitrariness is the more striking by comparison with the sixth Mass which uses the whole c.f. and divides it according to its natural phrases.

Here a comparison with earlier Masses is called for: for instance, the division of Leonel Power's Mass *Alma Redemtoris Mater* [28], one of the first cyclic Ordinary Masses written on a schematic c.f. which is repeated over and over again without any change. In Power's Mass there are probably structural reasons for this arbitrariness: the composer may have wished to divide the c.f. into two equal parts, in accordance with the English tradition

[28] *Documenta Polyphoniae Liturgicae S. Eccleciae Romanae*, serie I, no. 2, Rome 1947. (Ed. by L. Feininger).

of binary Mass movements. But on what principe was the division in these Masses effected? Possibly the composer was searching for motifs which after alteration and extension would serve as a base for the five Masses. However, the *L'Homme armé* song with its motion in intervals of fourths and fifths contains many varied forms of musical combination and any other division might equally well have stimulated the composer's imagination, without offending against the natural periodicity of the chanson. It appears that the division is determined by the textual structure, for if the composer had followed the musical logic, three possible divisions would have presented themselves:

a) I — L'homme, l'homme, l'homme armé; l'homme armé
II — l'homme armé doit on doubter
III — doit on doubter.

b) I — L'homme, l'homme, l'homme armé,
II — l'homme armé
III — l'homme armé doit on doubter; doit on doubter.

or even:

c) I — L'homme, l'homme, l'homme armé,
II — l'homme armé
III — L'homme armé doit on doubter
IV — doit on doubter.

But the composer followed the word units and grouped them together in the following order:

I — L'homme, l'homme
II — l'homme armé (3 x)
III — doit on doubter (2 x).

Thus structural function is conferred upon the secular text which determines even the basic material of every Mass, ignoring the inherent musical structure of the *L'homme armé* song.

2. The structure of the *cantus firmi* in the Masses

The sections of the chanson do not appear as *cantus firmi* in their original form but are treated as musical units upon which the composer elaborated so as to construct the scaffolding of the Mass. The elaboration consists of retrograde motion, inversion, transpositions of fourths and fifths and sequences. To the basic material of the single *cantus firmi* are added pauses whose constituent meaning is no less than that of the notes.

How closely the single phrases of the c.f. are interwoven as a result of this method of construction, is clearly demonstrated by the c.f. of Mass 2:

Ex. 3

The original chanson quotation (1) takes on three more forms: a - retrograde motion (R); b - inversion (I); c - retrograde motion and inversion (R I). All further combinations are derived from these:

2 =	R I of 1			
3 =	I ,, 1,	R of 2		
4 =	,, 1,	I ,, 2,	R I of 3	
5 (=1) =		R S ,, 2,	I ,, 3,	R of 4.

The following diagram demonstrates that each of the five — or actually four — sections stands in a threefold relationship to the others, thereby using all three methods of derivation.

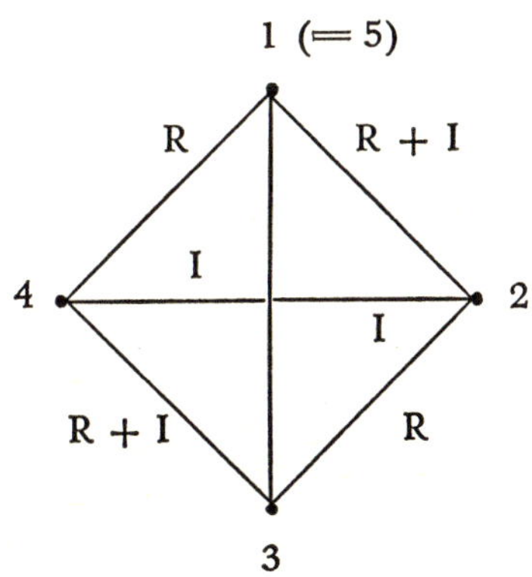

The way in which chanson sections are to be expanded into *cantus firmi* is indicated in each Mass by a canon always followed up with a *resolutio*. Below, the *cantus firmi* of the six *L'Homme armé* Masses are noted down and their development out of the chanson-quotation is shown:

Mass I:

Chanson excerpt:

Ex. 4

Canon: (1) Bis vicibus binis gradatim vir in ordine scandit
(2) Ut prius incessit, ipse retrograditur

Resolutio:

Ex. 5

Mass II:

Chanson excerpt:

Ex. 6

Canon: (1) Ambulat hic armatus homo (2) verso quoque vultu arma rapit; dexteram sequitur, (3) sicut vice versa ad lenam scandat. (4) Vultus sumendo priores ipse retrograditur: (5) respondent ultima primis.

Resolutio: See p. 27 ex. 3.

Mass III:

Chanson excerpt:

Ex. 7

Canon: (1) Sic metuendus eat (2) gressum rependendo ne pausat (3) demum scandendo per dyatessaron it (4) Ast ubi conscendit vice mox versa remeabit (5) Descensus finem per dyapente facit.

Resolutio:

Ex. 8

Mass IV:

Chanson excerpt:

Ex. 9

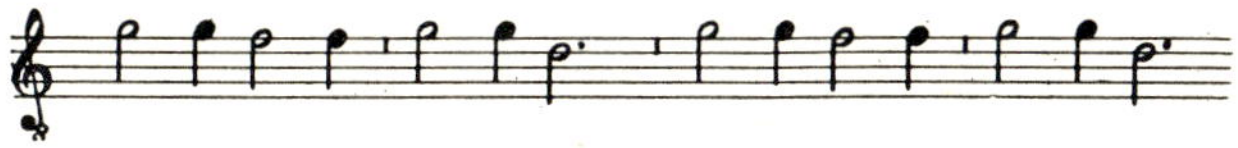

Canon: (1, 2): Buccina clangorem voces vertendo reflectit
(3, 4): Subque gradu reboat iterum clamando quaterno.

Resolutio:

Ex. 10

Mass V:

Chanson excerpt:

Ex. 11

Canon: (2) Per dyapente sonat subter remeando lorica
(3) Post ubi fimerit gressum renovando resumit.
(4) Tuque gradu sursum cantando revertere quinto
(5) Principio finem da qui modulavis eundem.

Resolutio:

Ex. 12

Mass VI:

Canon: Arma virumque cano vincorque per arma virumque
Alterni gradimur hic ubi signo tacet.
Sub lychanos hypaton oritur sic undique pergit
Visceribus propiis conditur ille meis.

Resolutio (refers to the emergence of a c.f. — Canon).

Ex. 13

This last resolution is not given in the MS. The end of the imitative voice is only marked by a *signum congruentiae*. The remark *sub lychanos hypaton*, it seems, is to be taken literally: below the *lichanos hypaton*. As the transcription shows, the canon does not begin on d (= *lichanos hypaton*) but on C (i.e. one note below the *lichanos hypaton*), and in this way a canon on the fifth below the c.f. originates (g in tenor I, C in tenor II). The two parts of the canon proceed in complementary motion, as the canon hints. The opening injunction of the canon *(arma virumque cano)* makes humorous reference to the beginning of Virgil's Aenid.

3. The constructive function of the c.f.

The c.f. appears once in every Mass Section containing a c.f., and is always stated in the tenor without variation. Nevertheless, it takes on three distinct basic forms which differ in measure and proportion. Here a process of diminution takes place: from the longest note values in *tempus perfectum* of the entry sections of the main movements (Model I), through the halved values in the *tempus imperfectum diminutum* of the middle sections (Model II), to the shortest values of the last sections of the movements, in *tempus imperfectum* (Model III) once again. Where the movement of a Mass is divided into more than three sections, the remaining ones are invariably without a c.f. The principle of shortened values, characteristic of that time, is adhered to here with but an occasional exception, even if at times relations other than those mentioned put an appearance. In Mass 3, for example, the measure of the last sections of the movement is C3 and not O; Mass 5 bears the sign C3 in the closing sections of *Osanna* and *Agnus*, and Ø in the last sections of *Gloria* and *Credo* movements.

Three different tenor models emerge: the entry sections of the main movements of the Mass follow Model I; the middle sections (where they contain the c.f.), Model II; and the closing sections, Model III. In Model III the c.f. appears in its *integer valor*, in Model II in twofold, and in Model I in threefold augmentation. There are exceptions in Masses 2 and 6, where the first sections of *Kyrie*, *Sanctus* and *Agnus* contain the c.f. in twofold augmentation. Additional exceptions occur in the *Sanctus* and *Agnus* movements of Mass 5 which do not end with Model III but with Model II, and the c.f. of Mass 2 never appears in its *integer valor*, but in augmentation of 2, 4 and 6.

It is obvious that the structure of the separate Mass sections is determined by the tenor scheme which serves as their basis. The measures and proportion of the tenor influence not merely the length of a section but also its internal division, the grouping of the voices and its harmonic style generally, as will be proved by examination of the mass movements and their structure.

The principle of the strictly repetitive, long-measured c.f. in the tenor is possibly derived from the isorhythmic motet. In two Masses, one by Leonel Power (*Alma redemptoris Mater*) [29] and one by Dunstable (*Da gaudentia praemia*) [30] the technique of the tenor motet seems for the first time to have been transferred to the Mass, since the tenor is stated twice in every movement. Dufay, in his *Caput* Mass, proceeds one step further: the c.f. of this Mass is presented in two models (O and ₵) which are repeated without variation in both sections of one Mass movement (here again, with the exception of the pauses at the beginning of a section and in its internal pauses). The *Caput* Masses of Ockeghem and of Obrecht use the same structural principle. In Dufay's *Se la face ay pale* [31], the tenor appears in three models, at least in *Gloria* and *Credo*, and the process of diminution is indicated by the canon: "Tenor ter dicitur. Primo quae

[29] *Ibid.* Cf. note 28.

[30] Cf. H. Besseler, *Bourdon und Fauxbourdon*, 152 ff.

[31] *Dufay* O III, 1.

libet figura crescit in triplo [= Model I], secundo in duplo [= Model II], tertio ut jacet [= Model III]." The Neapolitan Masses appear to be in agreement with this principle. The rigid use of the c.f. is not in itself indicative of an older technique. Oliver Strunk concludes that in the history of the c.f. Mass there are two distinct lines of development [32]: "... the strict and the free, the symmetrical and the asymmetrical, the one variation-like, the other 'durchkomponiert' ...". Both "go back to the very beginning of the development, just as they also continue to the very end". "Variation-like" c.f. Masses are, for instance, those of L. Power: *Alma Redemptoris Mater*; Dufay: *Se la face ay pale*; Josquin: *Hercules Dux Ferrariae* [33]; Palestrina: *Missa Ave Maria* [34]. All these Masses adhere to the principle of a fixed c.f., isolated from the other parts and proceeding slowly, also in cases where the tenor moves less rigidly. Of the *L'Homme armé* Masses the following belong to this category of c.f. Masses:

Dufay (c.f. slightly ornamented towards the ends of the sections);
Busnois (c.f. transposed in *Credo*, inversed in *Agnus*);
Caron (slightly ornamented);
Faugues (c.f. canon);
Regis (slightly ornamented);
Ockeghem (c.f. transposed in bass part of *Credo* and *Agnus*);
Basiron (principle of tenor model);
Vaqueras (c.f. canons, tenor models);
Obrecht (follows example of Busnois) [35];
Josquin (*super voces musicales*);
Pipelare (c.f. wandering, but always fixed in one part);
Carver (c.f. hovering between tenor and upper parts, yet always distinguishable from other parts by its slow motion);
Senfl (liturgical c.f. in the *superius*);
Palestrina (in five parts);
Morales (in four parts).

The rigid use of the c.f. in so many of the *L'Homme armé* Masses may be based on tradition, as Van den Borren observes: "... il est bien certain qu'en choisissant ce theme plutôt qu'un autre, les acteurs se sont

32 Review of the edition of Leonel Power's *Missa super Alma Redemptoris Mater*, *JAMS* II (1949), 107.

33 *Josquin MS*, II, 19.

34 *Opere Complete di G. P. di Palestrina*, Rome 1956, Vol. XXI, 142 (ed. by Casimiri).

35 On the relation between his Mass and that of Busnois see O. Strunk, "The Origin ...".

placés a un point de vue plus particulièrement traditionnel, donc en un certain sens retrograde" [36].

Although in the history of the Ordinary of the Mass the strict and the free treatment of the c.f. went side by side, it must be recognized that the general development of the c.f. tended towards greater flexibility. A few examples from different *L'Homme armé* Masses will serve to illustrate this development. As a first stage the c.f. shed its rigid form growing in similarity to the upper parts, at first only at the cadences (cf. Dufay's *L'Homme armé* Mass), later throughout its course (cf. Caron, Regis). Hand in hand with the "upward" development (*i.e.*, the assimilation of the part containing the c.f. to the upper parts), movement in a downward direction began to appear: motifs of the c.f. are taken over by the upper parts not only by way of anticipation but also simultaneously (cf. De Orto, Dufay). This innovation at first gives rise to a kind of Coloration Mass, whose parts all emanate from the idea of a c.f. which appears in paraphrased form (cf. the *L'Homme armé* Mass of Tinctoris — even if its c.f. is invariably confined to the tenor part; of Palestrina in four parts with altenarting c.f. technique). It is only later that the principle of through-imitation emerges: according to this the thematic material is imitated by all the parts, thus achieving thematic unity [37].

The c.f.-less inner movements, which tended to be strongly imitative, already formed a basis for subsequent through-imitation (cf. Obrecht and the Neapolitan Masses) as well as for the head imitation at the opening of Mass movements (cf. for instance Compère: *Kyrie* II; *Gloria* showing the beginning of through-imitation; Josquin *Sexti toni* — *Kyrie* I, *Agnus* I; Palestrina — in four parts — *Gloria*; and many movements of Obrecht's Mass).

In the final instance the through-imitated Mass became the main form in the sixteenth century. Consequently, if a sixteenth century Mass is found to be in "strict" style, it may be explained "als bewusste Nachahmung eines älteren Stadiums der Komposition oder als Denkmal besonderer technischer Gewandheit" [38]. Morales and Palestrina each composed a *L'Homme armé* Mass which represented the two different types of c.f. Mass [39]. From

36 *Etudes . . .*, 179.

37 Cf. *e.g.*, the article "Messe", *MGG* IX, 175.

38 P. Wagner, *Geschichte der Messe* I, Leipzig 1913, 73.

39 Cf. P. Wagner, *Ibid.*, 418. Morales' first Mass is written in four parts and the c.f. is strictly fixed in the tenor. In the second, five part Mass, the tenor pervades all

this point of view, therefore, no conclusions on the chronology of the Neapolitan Masses should be drawn.

Lastly, the Neapolitan *L'Homme armé* Masses are constructed according to two different principles of c.f. treatment. On the one hand they belong to the type of c.f. Mass with the secular borrowed c.f.; on the other, to the type of c.f. Mass with an independently conceived c.f., consisting of short melodic phrases. As in Josquin's Masses *Hercules dux Ferrariae* or *La-sol-fa-re-mi* [40], the c.f. of the first five Neapolitan Masses has no individual melodic character but is more structural in function, even if its basic material is taken from the *L'Homme armé* chanson. Only Mass 6 is an actual c.f. Mass on a borrowed tenor, this principle of composition being worked out to its ultimate conclusion in the cycle as a whole.

II. THE MOVEMENTS OF THE MASS

1. Internal division

The table below shows the division of the separate Mass-movements and the disposition of their parts. Missing parts, whose original existence may confidently be taken for granted, are given in parentheses and the number of parts each section is assumed to have contained, is indicated by a question mark. It is safe to surmise that *Kyrie* I and the last *Agnus* movements were written in four parts.

Comparison shows that there is analogy in those movements whose division springs naturally from the liturgical text. The *Kyrie* falls into three sections (the *Christe* being alternatively written for three and four parts), and the *Sanctus* into five: *Pleni* and *Benedictus* are textless throughout; *Osanna* is repeated *ut prius* except in Masses 1 and 3. The *Gloria* has three or four sections in which the points of division are analogous with those of the three part *Gloria* movements in Masses 1, 2 and 5 (and with small divergences, also in Mass 6). The *Credo* movements are divided into three to five sections. In Masses 4, 5 and 6 the last section begins with *Confiteor* while in Masses 1 and 3 it begins at *Et expecto* and in Mass 2 with *Et unam sanctam*. The *Agnus* movements fall into one to four sections, the fourth

voices. Contrary to Morales, Palestrina's five part *L'Homme armé* Mass is in strict style, while his four part Mass, written later, is in a free paraphrased technique.

40 *Josquin MS* I, 35.

Movts	Mass I		Mass II		Mass III		Mass IV		Mass V		Mass VI	
Kyrie	4 pts. (?) 4 ,, (?) 4 ,,	Kyrie I (O) [1] 54 [2] Christe [A, B (S, T ?)] Kyrie II	4 pts. (?) 3 ,, 4 ,,	Kyrie I (O) 59 Christe [S, A, B] Kyrie II	4 pts. (?) 4 ,, 4 ,,	Kyrie I (O) 64 Christe (Ȼ) 96 Kyrie II (O) 18	4 pts. (?) 3 ,, 4 ,,	Kyrie I (O) 60 Christe [S, A, B] (Ȼ) 60 Kyrie II (O) 32	4 pts. (?) 4 ,, 4 ,,	Kyrie I (O) 66 Christe (C_3) 66 Kyrie II (Ø) 36	5 pts. (?) 3 ,, 5 ,,	Kyrie I (O) 65 Christe = S, A, B (Ȼ) 92 Kyrie II (O) 34
Gloria	4 pts. 4 ,, 4 ,,	Et in terra (O) 54 Qui tollis Cum sancto	4 pts. 4 ,, 4 ,,	Et in terra (O) 87 Qui tollis (Ȼ) 174 Cum sancto (O) 30	4 pts. 2 ,, 4 ,, 4 ,,	Et in terra (O) 64 Domini fili, [S, A] (O) 32 Qui tollis (Ȼ) 96 Cum sancto (O) 18	4 pts. 3 ,, 4 ,, 4 ,,	Et in terra (O) 60 Dom. fili [S, A, B] (O) 30 Qui tollis (Ȼ) 63 Tu solus (O) 32	4 pts. (?) 4 ,, (?) 4 ,, (?)	Et in t. [S, T (A, B ?)] (O) 66 Qui tollis [A, B (S, T ?)] (C_3) 66 C. sancto [A, B (S, T ?)] (Ø) 36	5 pts. 5 ,, 5 ,,	Et in terra (O) 98 Domine Deus (Ȼ) 193 C. sancto (O) 34
Credo	4 pts. 3 ,, 4 ,, 4 ,,	Patrem (O) 54 Crucifixus [S, A, B] Et in spiritum Et expecto	4 pts. 4 ,, 4 ,,	Patrem (O) 87 Crucifixus (Ȼ) 174 Et unam (O) 30	4 pts. 2 ,, (?) 4 ,, (?) 2 ,, (?) 4 ,, (?)	Patrem (O) 64 Et incar. [S (A ?)] (O) 35 Et resur. [S, T (A, B ?)] (Ȼ) 96 Qui ex Pa. [A (S ?)] (Ȼ) 57 Et expecto [A, B (S, T ?)] (O) 18	4 pts. 3 ,, 4 ,, 4 ,,	Patrem (O) 60 Et incar. [S, A, B] (O) 32 Et ascendit (Ȼ) 63 Confiteor (O) 32	4 pts. 4 ,, 4 ,,	Patrem (O) 65 Crucifixus (C_3) 66 Confiteor (Ø) 36	5 pts. 5 ,, 5 ,,	Patrem (O) 98 Crucifixus (Ȼ) 193 Confiteor (O) 34
Sanctus	4 pts. 3 ,, 4 ,, 3 ,, 4 ,,	Sanctus (O) 54 Pleni [S, A, B] Osanna Benedictus [S, A, B] Osanna	4 pts. 3 ,, 4 ,, 3 ,, 4 ,,	Sa. (O) 59 Pl. [S, A, B] (O) 34 Os. (O) 30 Ben. [S, A, B] (Ȼ) 76 Os. (O) 30	4 pts. (?) 3 ,, (?) 4 ,, (?) 2 ,, (?) 4 ,, (?)	Sa. [S (A, B ?)] (O) 64 Pl. [S (A, B ?)] (Ø) 31 Os. [S, T (A, B ?)] (O) 32 Ben. [A (S ?)] (Ȼ) 61 Os. [A, B, T (S ?)] (O) 18	4 pts. 3 ,, 4 ,, 3 ,, 4 ,,	Sa. (O) 60 Pl. [S, A, B] (O) 41 Os. (O) 32 Ben. [S, A, B] (Ȼ) 74 Os. (O) 32	4 pts. 2 ,, 4 ,, 2 ,, 4 ,,	Sa. (O) 65 Pl. [S, A] (O) 28 Os. (C_3) 66 Ben. [S, A] (Ȼ) 54 Os. (C_3) 66	5 pts. 3 ,, 5 ,, 2 ,, 5 ,,	Sa. (O) 65 Pl. [S, A, B] (O) 40 Os. (O) 34 Ben. [S, A] (Ȼ) 72 Os. (O) 34
Agnus	4 pts. 3 ,, (?) 4 ,, (?) 4 ,, (?)	I (O) 54 II [S, (A, B ?)] III [S, T (A, B ?)] Dona [S, T (A, B ?)]	4 pts. 3 ,, (?) 4 ,, (?)	I (O) 59 II [S (A, B ?)] (Ȼ) 70 III [S, T (A, B ?)] (O) 30	4 pts. 3 ,, (?) 4 ,, (?) 4 ,, (?)	I (O) 64 II [S, (A, B ?)] (Ȼ) 60 III [S, T (A, B ?)] (Ȼ) 96 Dona [S, T (A, B ?)] (O) 18	4 pts. 3 ,, (?) 4 ,, (?)	I (O) 60 II [S, (A, B ?)] (Ȼ) 65 III [S, T (A, B ?)] (O) 32	4 pts. 2 ,, 4 ,, (?)	I (O) 66 II [S, A] (Ȼ) 57 III [S, T (A, B ?)] (C_3) 66	5 pts.	[S, T^1, T^2 (A, B ?)] (O) 65
C.f.	15 x		13 x		15 x		13 x		14 x		12 x	

[1] = time signature [2] = *Brevis* measures

separating the *dona nobis* from the rest of the text. In the *Agnus* movements, subdivided into several sections, a change in the number of parts is evident. The c.f., of course, is present in every section that contains the tenor; it appears three times in every *Gloria, Credo* and *Sanctus* while only once or twice in the external Mass movements. There is an exact analogy between the number of parts in the *Kyrie* and *Agnus* movements of Masses 1, 2 and 4.

2. Motto openings

The five movements in each of the six Masses bear the same opening mottos. There is a melodic affinity not only between the *superius* parts but also between the *contratenores*, while the tenor part rests at the beginning of each section. It is therefore possible to speak of a "stereotyped stratification" at the beginning of the main movements, whose motto openings (within each Mass) are all alike. After a few measures, often only upon the tenor's entry, the melody of each movement takes its own independent course. With the exception of Mass I, all the movements begin in 3 parts; only in Mass I, where the tenor part begins with 16 measures of rest, the opening is in the form of a duo between the three remaining parts, alternating between SA and AB.

In addition, there are often melodic affinities between the beginnings of the intermediate sections, even if less consistently than, for instance, in Dufay's *Missa ecce Ancilla* [41]. The middle section, written in *tempus imperfectum diminutum*, frequently is reminiscent of chanson-like motifs. Thus in the *Qui tollis* of the second Mass there is a quotation from the *L'Homme armé* chanson, using a motif which forms the basis of the c.f. of Mass 4. Sometimes reminiscences of the mottos of the main movements appear in the intermediate sections with different meters, as *e.g.* in Mass 4. At the beginning of final sections of movements, recurring melodic motifs are also found, although these are not exactly mottos. This unity is most obvious in Mass 6.

Taken as a whole, the unified and systematic motto opening is a salient stylistic feature of these Masses. The following motif, for example, frequently appears at the beginning of a number of sections:

41 *Dufay* O III, 66. See also Van den Borren, *Etudes* . . ., 151.

Ex. 14

The melodic line g-a-(g)-c-b-(a)-g may have been derived from the *L'Homme armé* chanson and here adapted to the traditional church mode [42]. The c.f. seldom furnishes the material for the motto: in Mass 6 (in the alto part); in Mass 5 (*Christe, Patrem*); and most strikingly in Mass 4, where the clearcut tenor motif appears in almost all sections that contain the c.f. This same motif appears even in Mass 2 (see above), the sole instance of a connection between a single Mass and a whole cycle.

3. The endings

The Mass sections frequently end with a closing formula intoned by one of the *contratenores*, while the superius and the tenor sing long-drawn notes. In all the Masses these formulae consist of similar melodic notes, i.e. primarily of pure or slightly elaborated triads.

Only in Mass 6 do the main movements close on the same final formula, thus creating a parallel to the beginning mottos and developing the final formulae in the manner of a *figura* as an *epistrophe*. The first four movements of the Mass all close in the same manner, adhering to the principle of "stereotyped stratification". All the voices participate in this procedure, each according to a fixed melodic progression. It is interesting to note that through the use of the final formula all the movements end on a *distonatio* [43], closing on the *finalis* of the second tenor part (c). The *distonatio* appears after the final cadence of the movement which ends clearly on g (the bass crossing the tenor after a *contratenor* clause). The

[42] A certain melodic affinity in the motto openings of many *L'Homme armé* Masses is very obvious. One should compare, for instance, the *superius* of the Masses of Dufay, Busnois, Caron, Faugues, Vacqueras and Brumel (who uses a motif similar to that of the Neapolitan Masses). Josquin (*super voces*) and De la Rue also use a similar motif, but in another mode.

[43] For the term *distonatio* cf. Tinctoris, *Liber de arte contrapuncti* III, chap. 5 (Couss. IV, 149).

subsequent movement begins on c (in the alto part), so that every movement actually comes full circle, beginning and ending on c above the lying note g in the tenor part. Only the *Agnus* which, in contrast to all the other Masses, is not subdivided at all, ends on the note g of the *finalis* in the bass. (Although the bass part is missing here, it may be reconstructed, tentatively at least, on the lines of the parallel sections using tenor model I).

There are other structural peculiarities in Mass 6. In *Gloria* and *Credo* similar final formulae appear also at the end of sections built on the identical tenor model, while the final formula of the *Sanctus* is reminiscent of the closing formulae of other Masses. The number 3 acquires a specific structural meaning: firstly, the movements, with the exception of *Sanctus* and *Gloria*, all consist of three sections, whereby the single *Agnus* movement is, as it were, compensated through the five sections of the *Sanctus*. Thus the sum total of the sections in this Mass amounts to 15 (= 5×3, that is to say, three times five movements). Moreover, the c.f. appears thrice in *Gloria, Credo* and *Sanctus* (this however is the case in the other Masses also) and in addition twice in the *Kyrie* and once in the *Agnus*. The outside movements of the Masses, therefore, complement each other and give rise to a numerical symmetry not found in any of the other Masses:

K	G	C	S	A
2	3	3	3	1
└─	─	3	─	─┘

Thus the c.f. is stated in this Mass twelve times in all, 12 being a figure to which a symbolical significance may be attributed.

The canon of the c.f., present in all the sections containing the tenor, has been previously mentioned. The two canonic parts are interwoven, the pauses in one part always filled in by the other. The c.f. is consequently present throughout a whole section (except for the pauses at the opening of a section), a fact which contributes to the musical integrity of this Mass.

III. THE SETTING

1. The function of the individual parts

Tenor. As has been shown, the central function of the tenor part in these Masses is emphasized by calligraphic means in the manuscript. A structural analysis of the Mass movements and their sections indicates the organic function of the tenor. The tenor conditions the whole structure:

its presence leads to a close-knit texture, to prevalence of the vertical elements and causes retardative movement; its absence means a longer texture, fluency of movement, the emergence of imitative or freer contrapunctal passages, a more liberal grouping of parts. The music appears constantly to alternate between full and thin voiced chords, between stagnation and forward movement, from the emphatic to the dynamic. These changes in tone colour are all the more impressive when we consider that the c.f. is performed instrumentally, whereas the c.f.-less passages are supposedly sung by soloists.

The *Superius* ranks second to the tenor part. Together with the tenor it constitutes the scaffolding of the setting. As the upper part, its melodic movement is often more elaborate, underlining and clarifying the text. Its ambit extends from b to g″ but does not usually exceed e″.

The *Bass* part, still called *contratenor* in these Masses, forms a counterpart to the tenor. Moreover, when the tenor drops out, the bass forms a counterpart to the *Superius, i.e.* as a substitute for the tenor part. Crossings of bass and tenor parts are frequent and in the 6th Mass even regular. Here the second tenor part moves into bass territory and at its entry the bass ascends into the upper octave leaving the fundamental rôle to the second tenor. *Contratenor* cadences often occur. Its ambit: B-f′.

The alto part here called *contratenor*, too, is the step child of the musical texture. It is merely a stop gap, does not take part in imitations and sequences and is, as it were, not permitted to take up the thematic material of the other parts. It is often overladen with text in order to obtain a more rational distribution of text in the other parts (cf. p. 17). The alto part often moves in leaps: intervals of a seventh are common. Nevertheless, the alto part has its own incipient motto at the opening of each movement. Its ambit extends from d to a′.

2. The grouping of the parts

The possibility of a freer grouping of parts only occurs in these Masses where the tenor pauses. Whenever the tenor is present, the setting is dense and homophonic; however, where it drops out, the remaining parts unite in forming duo or trio passages. The duos are always between *superius* and bass and the trios for the same combination with the addition of the alto. Such groups in fact only occur in sections based on tenor models I and II, where the tenor uses longer note values and where its rests are proportionally longer, permitting of such intermediate passages. In consequence it may be concluded that the grouping of the parts is dependent on the tenor structure, too.

The following table compares the tenorless and the tenor passages of the first sections of the *Gloria* and the *Credo* (tenor Model I) of Masses 1-5:

Mass	R	T	R	T	R	T	R	T	R	T	Total sum
I	16	8	16	8	changing	number	of	rests			16 T + 38 R
II	3	12	6	12	6	12	6	12	6	12	60 T + 27 R
III	8	16	8	16	8	8	—	—	—	—	40 T + 24 R
IV	4	8	8	8	8	8	8	8	8	8	40 T + 36 R
V	4	5	10	5	8	5	10	5	8	5	25 T + 30 R

R = rests; T = tenor measures.

From this table it is clear that in Masses 2, 3 and 4 the passages based on the tenor are longer than the tenorless passages, while Masses 1 and 5 comprise fewer tenor passages altogether. It is also important to note that within each Mass, the consecutive full and thin voiced passages are carefully balanced. Tenor and tenorless passages stand in a ratio of 1:2 (except in Mass 5), or even, as in Mass 4, in a ratio of 1:1. The pauses at the openings alone, *i.e.* at the introduction of a passage, amount to half the total number of pauses (with the exception of Mass I). Their duplication, then, is caused by the retrograde motion of the basic row (*i.e.* the c.f. quotation) with the pauses counted in, as we have seen above (pp. 27-29). The more complicated structure of Mass 5 derives from the upbeat of its c.f.

How does the composer exploit the regular interchange of tonal density, the outcome of his structural plan? Mass I shows that he does in fact strive to attain the greatest variety in his musical setting, whilst adhering to a definite scheme. For the *Gloria* and *Credo* movements of this Mass (tenor model I) the same pattern may be traced.

	8 m	8 m	8 m	16 m	8 m			
S	———		———	———————	———	changing	number	cadence
A	———	———	———	———————	———	,,	,,	,,
T			———		———	,,	,,	,,
B		———	———	———————	———	,,	,,	,,

The first 16 tenorless measures are split into two phrases, but subsequently at each tenor rest there are three part passages. The same pattern is followed in all the sections built on tenor model III, even if the smaller dimensions of these sections do not permit of any real episodes.

In Mass 2, too, this organized variety is felt. The intermediate tenorless passages are divided into three, the beginning and end consisting of three parts each, but the middle section alternating between duos of *superius* and bass or *superius* and alto. Care is taken in other movements of this Mass to avoid setting consecutive two parts passages for the same voice combination.

In Masses 3, 5 and 6 no two-part episodes occur within a passage for four parts (with the exception of one short passage each in Mass 3 and Mass 5). All the other tenorless passages in a tenor section are for three parts. Perhaps for this very reason, it is in these Masses especially, that whole duo sections are interpolated between tenor sections, thus compensating, as it were, for the lack of duo passages within the tenor sections themselves.

These three part interpolations are all tenorless, since wherever the tenor appears all the parts are present. They manifest the same structure and voice grouping throughout, proceeding through the whole vocal compass progressively from top to bottom, ending up by having all parts coming in simultaneously.

```
S ———          ———
A ———   ———    ———
B       ———    ———    (Cf. also p. 61 and note 81)
```

It is obvious from the foregoing conclusions that the grouping of the parts in these Masses is not conditioned by the text, but adheres to a strict scheme of construction. Within sections based on a c.f. freer groupings emerge only where the tenor rests; sections with a smaller number of parts are interpolated between sections with the full complement of parts, following the principle of *varietas*. Thus the *Pleni*, *Benedictus*, *Agnus II* and thrice the *Christe*, are composed for a small number of voices (*i.e.* 2-3 parts), a custom which had its point of departure already in the Masses of Dufay and which was observed well into the sixteenth century.

3. Short canons and imitations

Although it is inappropriate to speak of an imitative technique in these Masses, the compositions are often enlivened by the imitation of short canon passages.

Short canonical episodes appear almost exclusively where the tenor pauses. Usually these are duos between the *superius* and bass parts. The *alto* does not take part; it either rests or moves at a comparatively rapid, independent pace. Only in the tenorless sections written for two or three parts which tend generally to have a contrapuntal structure, does the alto join in the canons. A further exception occurs in Mass 2, where the alto sometimes participates in short canons as a third legitimate part. In Mass 3, too, we find a short canon with the participation of the alto part, and above a sustained tenor note [44]. These, however, are merely exceptions which confirm the rule [45].

Canons between *superius* and bass occur at an interval of a fifth or, more frequently, of an octave. Imitation begins at a distance of one to six *minimae*. There is no fixed order determining the entry of the voices.

The canons are not strictly carried through. Often, for example, they appear in chain form; a canon is developed to its end and, after a short rest (or often a short interlude containing the tenor part) starts off anew. Sometimes the interval between the two pars is diminished after that *caesura*. In another type of canon the second part, after a brief pause, assumes the lead whilst the first resumes as its imitator. Canons like these, which are comparatively common, constitute a special kind of "chain-canon" and might be termed as "cross canons". Example 15 (*Sanctus* of Mass 5, measures 54-61) shows the combination of several canonical movements typical of these Masses: at the beginning the *superius* imitates the bass at an interval of three *minimae*, then takes the lead and is followed by the bass at a distance of *one minima* (measure 56); finally (measure 58) the bass again imitates the *superius*, this time at an interval of a fifth. The parts then lead freely on into the cadence:

44 *Credo*, measure 39 ff.

45 For the canons in the Masses we may apply C. Van den Borren's statement: "L'imitation canonique ne disparaît point après de l'ars nova . . . Elle s'offre, d'autre part, avec des atténuations qui la privent jusqu'à un certain point de son caractère, dans les nombreux fragments de Messes à deux ou trois voix, datant principalement de la seconde moitié du XVe siècle et d'une partie du XVIe. Dans ces petits morceaux, la continuité propre à l'écriture canonique qui ont pour effet de la faire constituer en une succession de brefs canons d'une rigueur mitigée: mode de composition idéalement fait, au demeurant, pour compenser la pauvreté harmonique résultant de l'emploi d'un nombre aussi restreint de voix." Cf. "Quelques réflexions à propos du style imitatif syntaxique", *Revue Belge de Musicologie* I (1946), 14.

Ex. 15

Mass 5. Sanctus, m. 54 - 61

The melodic pattern of a canon is somewhat different from the melodic flow of the other passages. It generally works up to a climax, gradually retracing its steps back to the starting point. Less frequently it leads down from an immediate climax. An element of restlessness and forging ahead is characteristic of all the canonical melodies, possibly attained through gradual movement and rhythmic accentuation in the melodic line.

Besides the canon, imitations are also found in the Masses. At times it is hard to define the limits between canon and imitation. Since the canons, too, are often short, it is hard to say where the imitation stops and the canon begins. Generally speaking, the so called "canon" is not only longer than the transitory imitation, but it is also more rapid, rhythmically and melodically more significant and usually preceded and concluded by a cadence. Conversely, the "imitation" is imperceptibly woven into the musical fabric: it flits through some parts and fades out again. Unlike the canon, it does not give rise to new melodic material, using the material inherent in the movement. Almost all imitation juggle with triads, as is done in the final phrases, and whereas the imitation does at times rise above the tenor to be taken up by the alto, the canon does not. The imitations, which contribute to the unity of composition, are especially frequent in Mass 2, which indeed, in a sense, does not conform to the strict rules of composition prevailing in the other Masses. In example 16 (Mass 2, *Sanctus*, measures 33-35) a motif is imitated by three parts above a sustained note in the tenor:

Ex. 16

Mass 2. Sanctus, m. 33 - 35

The motif is repeated in this form, or with slight variation:

Ex. 17

13 times in this movement, mainly in the alto and bass parts. The motif — especially in its second form, on g — is taken from the motto of the movement and is also commonly used as a closing formula.

Twice in the Masses a motto is imitated, and it is interesting to note that the two places where this happens are similar: one is the beginning of the *Qui tollis* of the second Mass, the other the *Crucifixus* of the fifth. Both are middle sections on tenor model II. The second Mass, as has been mentioned, here uses the opening of the c.f. of the fourth Mass as a motto. This theme recalls the framework of the *Passamezzo antico* (Ex. 18, a) and is very suitable for such an exposition. In Mass 5 the imitated motif consists of two descending fourths, which again resemble a skeleton melody (Ex. 18, b). In each case the imitation is between *superius* and bass:

Ex. 18

Lastly attention should be drawn to the canon which runs through the whole of the sixth Mass. It is the imitation of the entire c.f. in the lower fifth, which is indicated through a directive canon, but not noted down. On the analogy of Faugues' *L'Homme armé* Mass, this too may be called *Missa ad fugam*.

4. Melodic sequences

Like the canon and the imitation, the melodic sequence in these Masses is in an early stage of its development. There are no sequential progressions, for instance, of the type that are found in Obrecht's *Missa libenter gloriabor* (*Kyrie* I) [46].

It is significant that the sequence, like the canon, appears only in the tenorless passages, even where it emerges independently and not in combination with a canon. In this respect several of the sequential progressions in the *Credo* of Mass 2 seem to be outstandingly "progressive". Example 19 (*Credo*, measure 68-72) shows a sequential movement which would appear to be typical of the sixteenth century, and which, moreover, is imitated in outline by the alto part:

Ex. 19

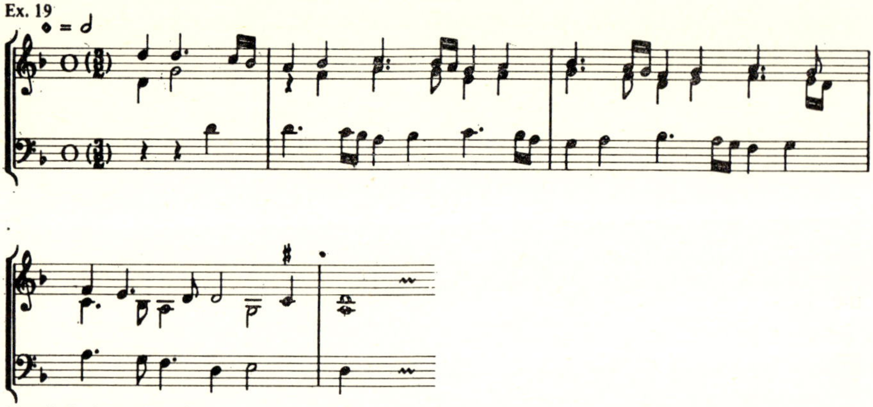

Mass 2. Credo, m. 68 - 72

Similar sequences, combined with canonic movement, also occur in measures 17 and 93 of the *Crucifixus*, these being the only clearly distinguishable canonic sequences of the Masses.

From the point of view of historical development a closer examination of the other types of sequences may be of interest. As stated previously, these appear only in c.f.-less sections and primarily in the lowest part. Their low position and their structure in fourths confer on them the character of scaffolding for the composition, and their place near the end of a section gradually leads up to a climax, in the nature of a "*stretta*". (Such a climax can be achieved through mere rhythmical repetitions, too, as e.g. in the *Benedictus* of Mass 2, where, towards the end, the rhythmical figure is repeated five times.)

Two illustrations may suffice: first the sequential movement of the bass part of the *Benedictus* of Mass 4, (example 20). The *superius*, here

46 *Van Ockeghem tot Sweelinck*, Amsterdam 1931, 53. (Ed. by A. Smijers).

Ex. 20

Mass 4. Benedictus, m. 32 - 37

the sole counterpart, circumscribes it with an individual, lightly disguised sequential movement. The opening of a new sequence in the *superius* is interrupted on account of the final cadence. The second example is the *Christe* of Mass 2, where the treatment of the sequence is especially ingenious (example 21). An ascending sequence in the bass, consisting of four links, is joined immediately by a similar figure inverted, twice repeated and leading on to the final note. Simultaneously, a three-fold sequential melody is stated in the *superius*, based on the inverted interval. The constructive element of the sequence in both parts is, only in that case, the interval of the third. The sequence is restless, rhythmically, in so far as it consists of group of five *minimae*, thus breaking out of the mensural unit. Harmonically, too, this sequence is unconventional: three bars prior to the final cadence the triad a-flat — c — e-flat is formed, so that the sequence threatens also to break up the mode:

Ex. 21

Mass 2. Christe, m. 32 - 37

This tonal extension again foreshadows future techniques, although it is not the result of consistent repetition (as e.g. the imitations in a circle of fifths in Obrecht's Mass *Maria Zart*), but is used merely as tone colour or to heighten the intensity [47].

[47] Other salient sequential progressions are: Mass 1: *Pleni, Benedictus*; Mass 2: *Christe*; Mass 4: *Benedictus*; Mass 5: *Pleni, Benedictus*.

The melodic sequences examined here still have an empirical air; they play with the tone material and experiment with melodic combinations. They appear more as means of driving the final cadence of a section, as an architectonic principle which, to speak with R. Lach, is used "wo die besondere Wichtigkeit einer Stelle für den Bau des Ganzen . . . ein scharfes Hervortreten solcher Dispositionsangelpunkte wünschenswert macht" [48].

IV. MELODIC STRUCTURE

The following examination was made on the basis of the melodic movement of the *superius* — melodically the leading voice.

The melodic line of these Masses is determined, as was usual in the 15th and 16th centuries, by stereotyped melodic formulae, which do not belong to the personal style of a single composer but to a whole generation. These are e.g. scales, *cambiate,* leaps in thirds, fourths and fifths and diverse cadence formulae.

Generally, the *superius* moves along broad melodic lines, often, in longer phrases encompassing as much as an octave. The movement may be downwards from a high point, or upwards (frequently in Mass 1) or even start from a central note expanding in both directions (as in Masses 2 and 3). The direction of movement is usually determined by the mode of the *superius* in each Mass. The melodic movement of the *superius* of Mass 1 is that of an authentic, of Mass 2 and 3 of a plagal mode.

All the Masses maintain a careful equilibrium between the direction of the movement and the position of the melody:

Ex. 22

Mass 1. Gloria, m. 1 - 8

In most cases the upward motion is rapid, a high note is reached in a leap, while the downward movement takes up more time, putting a restraint, as it were, on the dynamic energy:

[48] *Studien zur Entwicklungsgeschichte der ornamentalen Melopöie,* Vienna 1902, 9.

Ex. 23

Mass 3. Agnus, m. 5 - 9

The length of the phrases is varied, too, according to the principle of *varietas*. Short phrases are often paired, followed by longer phrases. This applies mainly to the *Gloria* and *Credo* movements and may be conditioned by the text.

In Mass 6 the phrases are somewhat shorter, their ambit is smaller and the development more restricted. The constant presence of the c.f. in this Mass seems to inhibit an independent melody. This shortcoming is, however, redeemed by a quick, nervously syncopated, rhythmic movement. In Mass 2 chanson-like motifs are conspicuous and gain in importance through repetition (cf. p. 69).

One motif recurs in all the Masses, the one mentioned above

Ex. 24

The same motif is found in the works of Dufay (frequently, e.g., in his Masses *l'Homme armé* and *Ave Regina Coelerum* [49]), Ockeghem, Busnois and their contemporaries [50]. Other forms of triad melodies occur, too. Consistently prominent are the canon passages, whose melodic course is always distinguished from the rest of the composition (see above).

We cannot, therefore arrive at any conclusion concerning authorship on the basis of melodic analysis. If, for example, certain "Dufayisms" are displayed in the mottos of Masses 1 and 6 (cf. Dufay's *Se la face* and *Ave Regina Coelerum*), this may be merely a matter of analogous modal structure (c-mode in Dufay and in Mass 1; predominant also at the beginning of the movements of Mass 6). Other motifs, such as triad melodies and pentatonics (cf. the above mentioned motto of the intermediate sections) and a number of general stylistic features are typical of these Masses as of the compositions of the Franco-Flemish circle as a whole. The strict structural plan underlying the Masses further hampers the melodic

[49] *Dufay* O, III, 91.

[50] Compare also with Dunstable's "English motto", cf. article "Dunstable", *MGG* III.

progression and makes it hard to decide whether their style should be termed "archaic" or "archaizing".

V. PROBLEMS OF TONALITY

1. Determination of tonality

Following the habit of the music theorists of the fifteenth and sixteenth centuries, we must determine the tonality of a polyphonic composition according to its tenor. The polyphonic composition (in the literal sense of the word *componere*), is conceived as a juxtaposition of different melodic lines: "Missa aliqua vel cantilena vel quaevis alia compositio fuerit ex diversis partibus diversorum tonorum effecta" [51]. These *diversae partes* are held together by the tenor: "... si quis peteret cuius toni talis compositio esset, interrogatus, debet absolute respondere secundum qualitatem tenoris eo quod omnis compotitionis sit pars principalis et fundamentum totius relationis."

The tonality of a given tenor is not, however, determined solely by its ambit and its *finalis*, but also by the melodic inflection typical of every mode. But where this Mass cycle is concerned, only the tenor of Mass 6 displays distinguishable modal character. The remaining *cantus firmi* are merely artificially constructed skeletons devoid of characteristic modal traits. Hence, in order to determine their tonality, it is essential to consider the other parts, too.

First, Mass 6 which is based upon the whole *L'Homme armé* chanson: The chanson is in the Mixolydian mode presenting all of its characteristics. To quote Cochlaeus: "Quinta ex G in d et rursus tercia ex d in iterum resiliens in d frequenti celebrantur usu in cantu septimi toni, quae eam ab causam diligentius notande sunt" [52]. The oscillation between d′-g and g′-d′ is also characteristic of the *L'Homme armé* chanson. Judged by the tenor, Mass 6 is written in the seventh mode [53].

[51] Tinctoris, *Liber de natura et proprietate tonorum*, chap. XXIV (Couss IV, 29).

[52] "De vera et infallibili tonorum agnitione", from his *Musica*, Cologne 1508. Quoted after B. Meier, "Die Handschrift Porto 174 als Quelle zur Tonartenlehre des 15. Jahrhunderts", *MD* VII (1953), 179.

[53] The seventh mode appears also in the c.f. used in the Masses of Carver, De Orto, Mouton Ockeghem, Palestrina and De la Rue, as well as in the chanson of Morton, of the *Mellon Chansonnier* and of the Basle MS. In nineteen other *L'Homme armé* Masses the c.f. apears in the following modes:

g Dorian: Basiron, Brumel, Busnois, Caron, Dufay, Faugues,
Tinctoris Vacqueras.

This tonality is not adhered to by the other Masses but preserved in Mass 6 alone, so that the whole cycle is not in fact written in the mode of the song, though ending in it. The other five Masses are written in the following modes (according to the *finalis* of their tenors):

Mass II:	*Finalis* d′ ,	Ambit	g-g′	(+b♭)	=	Mode	2.
Mass III:	,, f ,	,,	f-g′	(+b♭)	=	,,	5.
Mass IV:	,, d′ ,	,,	a-g′		=	,,	2.
Mass V:	,, d′ ,	,,	g-a′	(+b♭)	=	,,	2.
Mass I:	,, c′/g,	,,	g-f′		=	,,	7 or 11.

In Mass 1 there is some difficulty in determining the mode on the basis of the *finalis* of the tenor: According to the scheme of the c.f. the tenor ends on the note g, to be followed by an indefinite number of rests, after which the tenor enters, joining the final chord of the section with the double note $\substack{c\\g}$:

Ex. 25

Mass 1. Sanctus, m. 51 - 54

All the other parts, including the bass, end on c. Although g is the lower note and although, judging from the horizontal aspect, it should rightly be regarded as the *finalis* of the tenor; the addition of the note c to the final chord clearly shows that in the conflict between g and c in this Mass, the latter is victorious. This is a classic, indeed a deliberate case of *disgressio toni*. It should be remembered that Mass 6, too, inclines towards the c-mode, which means that entire cycle is framed by two Masses which move ambivalently between c and g, the first Mass ending on c and the sixth on g.

It follows from the different positions of the other parts, that they cannot conform to the tonality of the tenor, and that this gives rise to deviations — in the range of the authentic — plagal modes, at least. Gla-

d Dorian: Josquin (*super voces*), Palestrina (4 parts), Pipelare, Regis, De la Rue.
e Phrygian: Compère, Morales (4 parts), Obrecht.
a Phrygian: Senfl.
Lydian: Josquin (*sexti toni*), Morales.

reanus expressly says: "Hoc enim fieri videmus, quoties Hypodorii instuititur Tenor, ut eius Basis sit Dorius. Cantus ac Altitonans aliquando mement cum Tenore, aliquando evariant. Item, cum Mixolydius in Tenore est, Cantus ac Basis Hypomixolydii . . . systema habent" [54]. These divergencies tend to grow farreaching, particularly when it is found that in Masses 2, 4 and 5, the *finalis* g of the bass and of the *superius* part stand in contraposition to the tenor *finalis* g. The insertion of the b-flat, however, prevents a shift into the eighth mode, and the bass and *superius* parts remain in the second mode ex g. Such a transposition of a fifth is already authorized by Tinctoris as *finis irregularis*.

The following table compares the modal deviations of the four parts (*N.B. The licentia tonorum*, i.e. the exceeding or curtailment of the tone compass of a mode has not been taken into consideration).

	TENOR	SUPERIUS	BASS	ALTO
Mass I	7	11	11	12
Mass II	2	2 (ex g)	2 (ex g)	1 (ex g)
Mass III	5	6	6	8 (ex c)
Mass IV	2	2 (ex g)	2 (ex g)	7
Mass V	2	2 (ex g)	2 (ex g)	1 (ex g)
Mass VI	7	8	8	7

Tenor and bass twice appear in the relation of authentic plagal, three times in downward transposition of one and the same mode, and once (Mass I) in two different modes. If the somewhat anachronistic definition "eleventh mode" were to be replaced by the definition" eighth mode with close on the *confinalis* c", as the theorists of the late fifteenth century would presumably have put it, this Mass, too, would have been included in the same authentic plagal relationship.

After this analysis along contemporary criteria, the question of vertical harmony begs attention. As Bukofzer notes: "The musical result of his [Tinctoris'] 'compositio' produces, however, intervallic combinations which transcend the conception of mode and lead into the realm of harmony in a large sense" [55]. However, the musical theorists of the fifteenth and sixteenth centuries had not yet arrived at this conclusion. The last

54 Glareanus, *Dodecachordon* III, 13. Quoted after B Meier: "Zyklische Gesamtstruktur und Tonalität in den Messen Jacob Obrechts", *AfMw* X (1953), 301.

55 *Studies in Medieval and Renaissance Music*, 290.

anachronistic protagonist for the horizontal determination of tonality, Glareanus, demands that each part be analyzed separately. The earlier theorists did not go that far: Tinctoris determines the tonality of a composition from the tenor, Adam von Fulda formulates a minimum demand, that at least one part of the polyphonic composition should bear a modal character [56], Cochlaeus, in his *Musica Activa*, argues that a *tonus* is only an attribute of the tenor, the latter being a pre-existent monophonic melody [57]. Yet his examples of the formulation of cadences show that even if his cadences are conceived as the results of fixed melodic progressions, the bass part unquestionably plays the rôle of a fundamental voice [58].

The determination of tonality in these Masses may prove a small contribution to the problem of vertical versus horizontal. The vertical image agrees with the horizontal wherever the tenor and bass parts stand in a mixed authentic and plagal relationship to one another, i.e. wherever they have a common *finalis*. In Masses 2 and 5, however, the note g, which emerges from the vertical setting, always leads predominantly towards the final cadence, whereas in the intermediate cadences the notes g and d appear on equal terms. It is only towards the end of a section that the scales are tipped in favour of an "overall tonality", the final note of the tenor being interpreted as a fifth above the *finalis*, which appears in the bass. In Masses 2, 4 and 5 this tonal hesitation may be the outcome of the unnatural melodic structure of the tenor. In Mass 6, however, the *superius*, alto and bass parts in the main movements close on c, again an "interpretation" of the *finalis* g contained in the tenor. The fact that this treatment functions as a *figura* undoubtedly betrays the presence of a vertical consciousness, without which this ending could not possibly have been used as a deliberate artistic device.

Lastly, throughout Mass 1 there is a conscious sense of tonal ambiguity. Here two final notes are appended to the tenor, analogous to the *finales* of the vertical and horizontal lines. This "compromise" on the part of the *cantor* contradicts the rules laid down by the *musicus* and favours an overall determination of tonality.

56 "Tonus est . . . cognitio principii et finis, ascensus ac descensus cuius libet melodiae regularis". *Musica*, 1490. (Gerbert, *Scriptores* III, chap. 13, 354b).

57 B. Meier, "Die Harmonik im c.f.-haltigen Satz des 15. Jahrhunderts", *AfMw* IX (1952), 27.

58 *Ibid.*, 28. The conclusion, that Cochlaeus in his cadences considers also the vertical aspect, is not consistent with that of the author cited.

2. The cadences

The formation of the internal cadences may throw some light on the problem of tonality in the Masses.

Concentrating on the Mixolydian mode, the predominance of the fourth degree at once becomes obvious. In Mass 6 the majority of the cadences are on g, then on c and far fewer on d:

	C	d	F	G	a	B
Gloria	9	4	1	11	3	—
Credo	5	4	1	17	5	1
Sanctus	5	1	2	5	—	—
	—	—	—	—	—	—
	19	9	4	33	8	1

As previously stated, every movement of Mass 6 starts afresh from C and it is only at the tenor entry that it changes to G. This picture accords with the results of an examination of several rondeaux by Dufay and of madrigals and motets by Lasso, about which G. Reichert reports the following [59]: In Mixolydian rondeau compositions of Dufay the intermediate *caesura* invariably occurs on the fourth degree "mit der die Stücke auch gern beginnen". In secular Mixolydian compositions by Lasso the order of importance — according to Reichert — is I, IV, V and II and this tallies with the conclusions drawn from Mass 6. In the Dorian compositions of Dufay, on the other hand, the fifth degree generally prevails and in Lasso's, the degrees I, V and III. The picture which our Dorian Masses (on g) present is similar:

	g	a	B	C	F	d	
Mass II	29	3	7	—	3	25	(*Gloria, Credo, Sanctus*)
Mass V	13	5	5	—	3	15	(*Credo, Sanctus, Agnus*)
Mass IV	26	2	—	17	—	19	(*Gloria, Credo, Sanctus*)

(Owing to parts missing in Mass 5, it was not possible to examine parallel movements).

Only in Mass 4, where a b-flat is but rarely indicated and which therefore seems to oscillate between the Dorian and the Mixolydian modes, does the fourth degree gain in importance. In Masses 2 and 5 the predo-

59 "Kirchentonart als Formfaktor in der mehrstimmigen Musik des 15. und. 16. Jahrhunderts", *Mf* IV (1951), 35.

minance of the first and fifth degrees is unshaken. Finally, it should be noted that the third degree often takes on the character (to the modern ear) of a "delusive cadence", i.e. it appears as a substitute for the fifth degree or as a postponement thereof, mainly where the tenor rests [60].

In comparing the schematic construction of these Masses we may enquire: Where do the cadences appear? Are parallels perceptible between the internal cadences of different sections, belonging to the same tenor model? Do analogous cadences appear at similar points of the c.f. part? Upon examination it is found that none of this happens. An identical "realization" of a given tenor note, be it as a cadence or as an ordinary chord, forms an arbitrary exception. The converse is true: it seems that the composition aims at *varietas* both in the consecutive flow and in the simultaneous combination of tones. It may, however, be observed that within one model certain tenor notes (e.g. a longer note or the first tenor note after a rest) are often used as "anchorage points" and moulded into a cadence. Thus, in sections on the same tenor model an equal number of cadences are found and those most often in identical places, although the chords are different in themselves. A specially striking parallel exists in Mass 5, where cadences are formed at almost analogous points even in c.f.-less passages. Examination of the opening phrases of the *Credo*, *Sanctus* and *Gloria* movements reveals that on four occasions the same chords result, be it in c.f.-less sections (bars 10/11; bars 30/40/41), or over a given tenor note (bars 20; 48).

Melodically we find every type of cadence. It is significant that tenorless passages contain almost exclusively leading note cadences (with leading note in the *superius*) and Phrygian cadences, whereas in passages containing the c.f., all kinds of cadences occur, such as the underthird, sliding note and contratenor cadences [61].

The final cadences of the movements consist of simultaneously sounding perfect consonances. However, in a number of inner sections a third is inserted into the last chord, always as an additional note, splitting the alto or bass parts, but never the tenor or the *superius*. The bass mostly ends on the *contratenor* clause, even in places where the pendulous movement between degrees I-V on the melodic line of the bass is particularly

[60] See also E. Apfel, "Zur Entstehungsgeschichte des Palestrina Satzes", *AfMw* XIV (1957), 40.

[61] Terminology partly after B. Meier, "Die Harmonik:. . .".

apparent. A final cadence V-I, almost modern in form, is found in Masses 1, 3 and 4.

To sum up our conclusions about the problems of tonality in the six Masses: It would be exaggerated to speak of "tonality" as of a succession of functionally related chords. Nevertheless, there is a pronounced tendency towards a tonic, consolidated by a leading note cadence in the *superius* and by a movement between D-T in the bass, especially at the close of movements and sections. The following is a typical example of a closing formula:

Ex. 26

Mass 5. End of Credo

Although every part examined separately has its own modal shape, the final cadence always indicates an overall sense of tonality, in which the vertical elements predominate. True, the tonality of a work is determined by the tonality of its c.f.; the internal cadences, too, are a projection of the tenor part [62], yet the bass here clearly joins the fundamental tenor-*superius* combination, to weld all parts — especially towards the end of a movement — into a fixed tonal framework [63]. If the final note of the bass part is identical with that of the tenor, the gap between tonality is bridged in a natural manner. What would happen if the final notes differed? The theorists of the fifteenth and sixteenth centuries state it is the tenor part alone which determines the tonality of a composition. The theory of the church modes is still so firmly entrenched in the theoretical thought of the time that the conscious vertical examination of a composition is unthinkable for theorist and composer alike. Morales and Palestrina still determine the tonality of their works according to the tonality of the tenor, and e.g. the edition of Lasso's work by Le Roy and Ballard (Paris, 1565) groups the compositions together according to their tonality, i.e. the tonality

62 Cf. B. Meier, *ibid.*

63 It is significant, that already Gafurius had extended Tinctoris' statement about the rôle of the tenor (cf. above p. 48), saying: "... Tenorem vero, quod cantum sustinet et a Baritonante sustinetur fundamentum relationis dicunt", (*Practica Musicae*, Milano 1496, chap. III, 15).

of their tenor parts. Even Zarlino who recognizes the fundamental function of the bass part, who equates the bass to the "earth" and who requires that it alone close on the tonic of the mode [64], in another book evades this modern concept, stating that the tenor determines the tonality of a compositions and its basic mood [65].

Yet, all this does not prove the complete absence of a sense of overall tonality, for as was shown in the examples, especially in those from the first and sixth Masses, in compositions of the fifteenth and sixteenth centuries a modern vertical concept of tonality already begins to make itself felt. S. Hermelink's words about the musical theory of the sixteenth century would equally apply to the late fifteenth century: "Offenkundig tritt hier zutage, dass die traditionelle Tonartenlehre die wirklichen Verhältnisse, welche in der ausgereiften Vokalpolyphonie herrschen, nur mangelhaft zu umgreifen vermag" [66]. It is in the fifteenth century that theory and practice begin to diverge, although the contemporary composers and theorists may not have been aware of it. The result is the compromise between the horizontal and the vertical as laid down in these *L'Homme armé* Masses.

3. Harmony

Comparison of the various vertical chords above the notes of the c.f. is again facilitated by the analogous structure of the composition. As the c.f. is repeated according to a rigid, invariable pattern, a comparative table of the vertical "realization" (to avoid the term "harmonization") of the tenor notes was drawn up. As the vertical chord of the late fifteenth century consists of perfect and imperfect consonances, every note of the tenor may be interpreted as root, fifth or third. Comparison shows that Mass 6 exploits almost all the possibilities.

g	appears as Root note in chord	G,	Fifth in chord	C,	Third in chord	e.
a	,, ,, ,, ,, ,, ,,	(a),	,, ,, ,,	d.	,, ,, ,,	F.
b	————————	,	,, ,, ,,	e,	,, ,, ,,	G.
c	,, ,, ,, ,, ,, ,,	C,	,, ,, ,,	F,	,, ,, ,,	a.
d	,, ,, ,, ,, ,, ,,	d,	,, ,, ,,	G,	,, ,, ,,	B.
e	————————	,	,, ,, ,,	a,	,, ,, ,,	(C).
f	,, ,, ,, ,, ,, ,,	F,	,, ,, ,,	a,	,, ,, ,,	d.

(Chords in parentheses point to a rare use of the note)

64 *Istituzioni Harmoniche*, Venice 1562, chap. 59, 243.

65 Quotation in S. Hermelink, *Dispositionis Modorum*, München 1960, 59.

66 *Ibid.*, 12.

As far as harmony is concerned, the settings of the Masses follow the rules laid down by Tinctoris. Dissonances appear only as suspension notes or as passing notes, the maximum value of the latter never exceeding a *minima.* A salient example, for instance, is the closing formula of the movements in Mass 3, where a dissonance occurs on the penultimate (albeit after the final cadence). Passing dissonances of this kind are found in other places in the Masses, too. They seem to stem from the compulsion exercised by a melodic movement which looks upon vertical accord as a matter of secondary importance. In spite of this, the setting is on the whole devoid of dissonances. To some extent Mass 6 is an exception. Here dissonances are more frequent but not, it seems, for reasons of heightened expression nor due to a combination of individual melodic lines, but owing to a certain carelessness on the part of the composer as he approaches the end of the plan, or on the part of his copyist.

Suspension notes are mostly resolved by degree progression, sometimes — though rarely — through a downward leap of a third, a forerunner of the *cambiata* [67]. Parallel fifths and octaves in all parts are circumvented by means of syncopation, as in the following example:

Ex. 27

Mass 3. Credo, m. 7

Fauxbourdon progressions in particular precede candences. Parallel thirds and sixths frequently occur between *superius* and bass, or between *superius* and alto parts.

When the c.f. part is present the progression is limited, as we have said, mainly to chords of thirds and fifths, which means relative stagnation of movement. Chords are strung together successively without relation to each other: They arise as "realization" to the tenor notes. Thus we find *varietas* in two ways: First in the interchange between contrapuntally dynamic and euphonically static passages (which goes hand in hand with the interplay between thin-voiced and full-voiced writing). Secondly,

[67] Thus K. Jeppesen interprets this progression in the historical introduction to his *Counterpoint,* New York 1939, 16-17.

within the homophonic passages, in the striving towards varied interpretation of the notes of the c.f.; and, in the contrapunctal passages, in the manifold ways of grouping the voices, of periodization and of setting, e.g. canonical interludes, counterpoint, parallel movement, *etc.*

VI. THE RELATION BETWEEN WORDS AND MUSIC

As implied by the somewhat arbitrary setting of the text, the direct allusion to the word is extremely vague in the six Masses. Even the phrase *ascendit in coelum* which was set in a descriptive manner in an early *Credo* movement by Jean Francois [68] — a technique later adopted by Dufay (*Missa Ave Regina Coelorum*) [69] and by a whole generation of fifteenth and sixteenth cent. composers — even a phrase such as that does not create any musical symbolism. In Mass 5 it is, in fact, set to an ascending musical phrase but in Masses 1 and 2 it is set to a descending line. *Noema* symbols, as e.g. in Machaut's Mass [70] on *ex Maria virgine*, in Arnold de Lantins' Mass *Verbum incarnatum* on *Amen* (at the end of the *Gloria* and *Credo*) [71], or in Dufay's *Ecce Ancilla* [72] at the end of the second *Kyrie*, are not found. The contrary is true: central verbal passages are sometimes set to a double text so that the words lose their individual value altogether.

If, nevertheless, one can speak of a relationship of text to music in these Masses, it is neither in tonal description nor in musical symbolism. In movements containing a good portion of text there is a kind of recitation melody which differentiates between separate sentences (e.g. Mass 1, *Credo*; Mass 5, *Credo: genitum, Qui propter nos*; Mass 6, *Gloria, Credo: factorem coeli*). The declamatory part is usually given to the *superius*, often imitated by the bass. The melody of these passages is characterized by tone repetition and short phrases following closely upon one another. The *Credo* of Mass 6 (bars 4-7) with its striking tone repetition on e″ is a good example:

ex. 28

68 *Polyphonia Sacra*, London 1932, 99 (ed. by C. Van den Borren), under the name J. Franchoys. See also Van den Borren *Etudes*, 108.

69 *Dufay* O, III, 91.

70 *Polyphonic Music of the Fourteenth Century*, Monaco 1956, III, 37.

71 *Polyphonia Sacra*, 14, 23.

72 *Dufay* O, III, 66.

In Mass 1, the text between *Et in unum Dominum* and *unigenitum* is broken off in four places and set in a kind of "terrassed" melodic style which gradually encompasses the entire octave. The whole *Credo* movement of Mass 1 is characterized by short, mosaic-like phrases.

This melodic movement has an archaic air. The "déclamation rapide et martelée" [73] for instance, is found in the Mass movements of Arnold de Lantins especially in the *Kyrie* and the *Credo* of his above mentioned *Missa verbum incarnatum*, and in the earlier four part Masses of Dufay (*Caput* [74] and *Se la face*). But whereas Dufay and Lantins know how to adapt this declamatory melodic line to the text and how to attain the desired emphasis of central passages, phrases or words of the text, the same does not hold good for our Masses. Here the melody is scarcely a derivative of the text and of its interpretation, but seems rather to follow an autonomous musical logic. According to this logic, intensification is achieved through the interchange of short and long phrases, and of "repercussive" bow-phrased melodic links [75]. In addition, the stronger declamatory character of the *Gloria* and *Credo* movements is undoubtedly explained by the richness of their texts. For if we remember that all the Mass movements are based on the same tenor scheme and that accordingly phrases rich and poor in text respectively are of equal length, then it is small wonder that some turn out to be syllabic and others more melismatic.

If it is permissible to speak of symbolic motives in the Masses at all, they should be sought in the construction: the threefold repetition of the whole c.f. in the *Gloria* and the *Credo*, the three tenor models which form the basis of each Mass and last but not least — the climax in Mass 6, attained not only by the addition of a fifth part, but also by the numerical relationships described above.

This aspect is of great significance for the style of the Masses, whose focal point is their construction.

73 H. Pirro, *Histoire de la musique de la fin du XIVe siècle à la fin du XVIe*, Paris 1940, 69.

74 *Dufay* O, II, 75.

75 Even if in Mass I the words in *unum Deo* are musicaly symbolized, as it were, by the repetition of one note, the reoccurrance of the same motif in the text *qui propter nos homines* shows, that no symbolic meaning should be attributed to the motif.

VII. CONCLUDING REMARKS ABOUT STYLE

Any attempt to fix the date of the Masses on purely stylistic grounds is very problematic. Are the Neapolitan *L'Homme armé* Masses truly representative of contemporary style or are they *a priori* retrospective? Does what we term "regressive" in them point to a relatively early date of composition or is it a conscious stylistic element?

In order to get closer to a solution of these problems, it is advisable to sum up the stylistic constituents of the Masses under the headings of regressive or progressive. The seventies of the fifteenth century serve as our point of departure, since it is to this period that musicologists have until now ascribed the Masses.

Regressive stylistic elements

The first hint at archaism is the rigid schematic plan underlying the Masses. By this is not meant the strict, almost isorhythmic treatment of the c.f., for according to O. Strunk this treatment persists through the entire development of the Mass cycle up to the sixteenth century. (It should, by the way, be noted that after Dufay's *Se la face* and with the exception of the *Caput* Masses of Ockeghem [76] and Obrecht [77] which are based on tradition, there are actually no Masses with fixed c.f., where the c.f. is repeated so strictly and undeviatingly as in these *L'Homme armé* Masses.) However, in the main, the archaic impression is due to the technique of the tenor model which is so invariably adhered to that even the rests are included in the repeated *talea*, exactly in the manner of the isorhythmic motet. Further, the melodic and rhythmic isolation of the tenor part which — contrary to the other parts — progresses in long values and whose melodic motifs are but rarely taken up by the other parts, is reminiscent of earlier practice rooted in the isorhythmic tradition. The change of colour in the manuscript points in the same direction: the presence or absence of the tenor is indicated through a change of colour in the notation of all parts. Thus, its "splendid isolation" and its constitutive function in the Masses are emphasized. In his remarks to Dufay's *Caput* Mass which he dates circa 1440, H. Besseler states that the conscious concentration around the c.f. is an early stylistic feature: "The tenor is the key to the form, for its opening is clearly indicated in the upper voices by a 'Signum congruentiae'.

[76] *Ockeghem W* II, 37.

[77] Obrecht, *Missen*, Amsterdam 1908–21, IV, 189 (ed. by J. Wolf).

Characteristically, this sign is missing in the Kyrie" — which Besseler thinks was written later, in 1463 — "for by 1463, the tenor Mass must have become normal enough to dispense with it. When the first *Missa Caput* was first written however, the principle was new and therefore the entry of the tenor had to be specially marked" [78].

The central function of the tenor in these compositions gives rise to other characteristics of musical setting, all seemingly regressive. For example, the emergence of canonic and sequential passages above c.f. rests only, a rule also observed by Dufay, Busnois and Ockeghem, though by no means as strictly as in these Masses (or the greater part of them). The subordinate rôle of the alto part and its reluctant participation in canons seems also to lag behind the technique of Dufay, Busnois, Ockeghem and their contemporaries. The undifferentiated part grouping is significant, too: the tenor entry is always with a full complement of voices and duos between the tenor and another part never occur. This techniques conforms on the whole to that of Dufay, who nevertheless knew how to break it ingeniously (cf. *Missa Se la face — Confiteor; Missa Ecce ancilla* and *Regina Coelerum, passim*). In the notation the coexistence of two different *brevis-longa ligatures* is conspicuous. The endings are somewhat peculiar although they throw an interesting light on problems of tonality. It was Josquin who demonstrated in his *L'Homme armé* (*super voces*) Mass how the problem of disparate final notes could be masterly solved. The short, declamatory phrases of the *Gloria* and *Credo* movements also seem in a sense retrospective, as does the simultaneous word setting in some passages of these movements.

These arguments might suffice to adopt an earlier dating of the MS, if other stylistic features did not furnish us with conflicting arguments, contradicting the impression of archaism.

Progressive stylistic elements

In the first place, some sequential progressions, especially in Mass 2, deserve attention, for they stand out against the background of the general style of the Masses. Furthermore, the analogues endings of the movements in Mass 6 are a means of unification, to be elaborated only later by Josquin, even if more skilfully. Several experiments at head imitation in Mass 2, the occurrence of c.f. motifs as head motifs in Masses 4, 2 and 6 also contradict

78 *Dufay* O, IV, vi.

the archaic rules of composition which prevail elsewhere in the Masses. In regard to notation, the use of Ͼ as symbol of augmentation (and not of measure) may be a progressive element too, for this meaning, according to W. Apel, was given to it only after the time of Dufay [79]. A further indication for a later dating of the Masses is given by the recapitulation of the second *Osanna ut supra* in Masses 2, 4 and 6. For instance, Dufay always sets the *Osanna* twice, Ockeghem, on the other hand, once only, repeating it after the *Benedictus* [80].

Together with the progressive and regressive tendencies shown by the musical texture, we should mention those features which fit into the period around 1470. Here especially an affinity with certain stylistic traits of the late Busnois and Dufay is manifest. Some chanson-like episodes, on the other hand, are reminiscent of Busnois' Burgundian style (see below, p. 69). The melodic structure of the *superius* of Mass 1, on the other hand, at once calls into mind Dufay's melodic style, although this may be due to the use of analogous tonalities. The conspicuous character of the canonical episodes, which distinguish themselves from the rest of the movements, is also common to Dufay, Busnois and the Neapolitan Masses. As we have said, the episodes generally occur only when the c.f. rests.

The long introductory passages to the movements of the Mass also recall the tradition of Dufay, Busnois and to some extent also of Ockeghem, even if the division of the duo passages into the combination SA+AB, repeated over and over again, seems to be a "personal" feature of these Masses. The scheme

S	———		———
A	———	———	———
B		———	———

is especially typical of Dufay, although he indulges in a variety of combinations, while in our Masses this scheme is adhered to very strictly [81].

[79] Cf. *Die Notation der polyphonen Musik*, Leipzig 1962, 182. Of course this statement should not be taken too literally.

[80] The *Benedictus* in Ockeghem's Masses, by the way, is often divided into two sections; sometimes, on the contrary, it is included together with the *Pleni* and the two *Osannas* in a single, undivided *Sanctus* movement.

[81] In his Mass *Se la face* Dufay groups the voices of the three part sections in the following manner:

The combination of all these progressive, regressive and contemporary features proves that it is impossible to determine the exact date of the composition of the six Masses solely on stylistic grounds. Let us therefore return to the manuscript itself and to the indications which it contains and try to consider it in its historical and cultural context.

D. THE ORIGIN OF THE MASSES AND THEIR DATING

As stated at the beginning of this study, the last page of MS E VI 40 contains an epigram, which may enlighten us as to the date when the Masses were composed. The epigram is as follows:

Ad serenissimam Ungarie Reginam:

Regia progenies et regi nupta beatrix
Qua sub sole viget nulla probanda magis,
Te tua virtutum series lustrata per orbem
Nunciat, ut nostris sis quique nota locis.
Tu modo divinos cultus regionibus istis
Extollens, cantus aducis ipsa modos.
O pietas miranda nimis laudandaque, maius
Hoc regina tibi quod decus esse potest?
Rex hostes fidei vincit. Regina colendo
Magnificat sanctum sublevat atque fidem.
Quam bene concordi iunxerunt numina lecto
Quos natura facit moribus esse pares.
Hinc licet ignotus, dominam te munere tantam
Ausus adire fui, servulus ipse tuus.
Charolus hoc princeps quondam gaudere solebat
Conveniet, certum est, moribus idque tuis.
Hoc capias igitur quaeso, videasque libenter,
Munus ab ignoto saepe placere solet.
Jam valeas foelix cum caro coniuge semper
Augeat in nostram fortis uterique fidem.

Christe:	S	— — —		— — —	— — —
	A	— — —	— — —		— — —
	B		— — —	— — —	— — —
Pleni:	S	— — —	— — —		— — —
	A	— — —		— — —	— — —
	B		— — —	— — —	— — —
Benedictus:	S	— — —			— — —
	A	— — —	— — —		— — —
	B		— — —		— — —

Fol. 64. Dedication and blazon

[illegible] [illegible] et recti nimium beatus
Qu[illegible] sese vivet nulla [illegible] matris
Et tua virtutum series lustrata per orbem
Illuminat ut nostris sic quoque nota locis
In modo divinos cultus rationemque isthic
Excellens [illegible] aditus ipsa modo
O pietas miranda nimis laudanda [illegible] manus
Hoc regina tibi quod decus esse potest
Ex hoste fidei vincere [illegible] recolendo
Magnificat sanctam sublevat atque fidem
[illegible] bene concordi universae numina [illegible]
[illegible] natura facit [illegible] esse pares
Nunc licet ignotus dominum te munere tantum
Ausus adire sui servitutis ipse tuus
Exhibeat hoc [illegible] quondam mandere solebant
Convenit certum est moribus idque tuus
Hoc capias igitur quaeso vultus [illegible] libenter
[illegible] ab ignoto saepe placere solet
[illegible] foedus cum caro coniuge semper
[illegible] fortis utrique fidem

Translation (free):

To the illustrious Queen of Hungary:

Royal progeny Beatrice, happily married to a king, / there is no one beneath the sun fairer than thou. / The list of thy virtues, spread the world over, / speaks thy fame so far and wide that thou art known even in our parts. / Thou art the only one that bringest heavenly culture to those parts / and also tuneful melodies. / Oh, admirable piety, worthy of the highest praise / what could embellish thee, Queen, more than this? / The King conquers the enemies of the Faith. It is the Queen / who, with zealous care, enhances and sustains that sacred faith. / How wisely the gods united in the nuptial bed / those whom Nature had united in their ways of life. / It is this that has emboldened the lowliest of thy servants, unknown / to take the liberty of making an offering to such a sovereign lady. / As surely as Charles the Duke was wont to revel in it / may it prove gratifying likewise to thy taste. / Mayst thou deign to accept it and take pleasure in it, / A gift from one unknown often gladdens the heart. / May thou, furthermore, always live joyfully with thy beloved spouse / and may you both with steadfast courage grow ever stronger within our Faith.

The Queen in question was Beatrice of Aragon, Queen of Hungary. Beatrice of Aragon was the second daughter of Ferdinand I (Ferrante), King of Naples, and of his wife Isabella of Chiaramonte. Beatrice was born in 1457 and in 1476 married King Matthias Hunyadi I (Corvinus) of Hungary with whom she lived at his palace in Buda until his death in 1490. Later she secretly married to his successor, King Ladislaus II of Bohemia. In 1500 this marriage was annulled by Papal decree and in 1501 Beatrice returned to Naples and died in 1508 [82].

From early childhood Beatrice of Aragon had received a broad education, with emphasis on gymnastics, literature, plastic arts and especially on music. For at the brilliant court of the Kings of Aragon music was considered indispensable. Following the example of the Toscana, *sacre rappre-*

Within this variety there appear two principles which are typical of Dufay's voice grouping in three part sections: the section always starts with two voices and ends with three, and the direction of the parts, entering in couples, is always downwards. Ockeghem, for example, sometimes brings a three part section to its end with two voices only (*e.g. Missa De plus en plus, Pleni; Ecce Ancilla, Pleni; Mi-Mi, Pleni, Benedictus*). The movement in those sections of his Masses is often directed downwards (*e.g. L'Homme armé, Pleni; Ecce Ancilla, Pleni; Mi-Mi, Benedictus*). (All the examples are taken from *Ockeghem W*, I).

82 For a detailed biography see A. de Berzeviczy, *Béatrice d'Aragon, Reine de Hongrie*, Paris 1911. (2 vols.)

sentazioni, as well as *momos, balli* and *mascherate* were often performed in the large hall of the *Castello Nuovo* and in the churches of Naples [83]. These festivals were usually featured by vocal and instrumental music. Publicly celebrated, they were mainly intended for the nobles gathered around the court. Whereas at the time of Alfonso, Ferrante's father, the music at court had been entrusted to Italian and Spanish musicians, Ferrante engaged excellent musicians of the Franco-Flemish school. In 1474 (or 1475) Tinctoris was invited to Naples where he very likely had an important hand in the education of Princess Beatrice. Under Tinctoris musical life in Naples flourished. In his *Liber de arte contrapuncti* he introduces himself as *jurisconsulis, musicus et capellanus* [84]. He dedicated his treatises *De arte contrapuncti* and *Proportionale* to the king and his *Complexus effectum musices, De regulari valore notarum* and *Diffinitorium* to Beatrice. In the introduction to *Diffinitorium* he praises Beatrice's musical talent: she seeks in music relaxation from her preoccupation with poetry, rhetoric and the fine arts, enriching her musical education: ". . . non modo deductionem in omni suo genere per alios . . . sed etiam per te ipsam assumens" [85]. In his *Liber de arte contrapuncti* Tinctoris sets the following text to a musical example: *Beatissima Beatrix/ prudens virtutum amatrix/ nos omnes abs te amatos/ in eternum fac beatos* [86].

When, after her marriage to King Matthias Corvinus in December 1476, Beatrice went to Hungary she found musical conditions there not inferior to those she had left. The court of Buda, too, was imbued with ideas of Western culture and there, too, the art of music was especially cultivated [87]. Already at the wedding ceremony in Buda the foreign guests admired the outstanding choir which performed at Mass. Later, in 1483, the Papal nuncio informed the Pope in Rome that the choir of Buda,

83 Cf. I. Pope, "La Musique Espagnole à la Cour de Naples dans la seconde moitié du XVe siècle", *Musique et Poésie au XVIe siècle*, Paris (1954), 35 ff.

84 *Couss.*, IV, 76.

85 *Ibid.*, 178.

86 *Ibid.*, IV, 138-39.

87 On the music at the court of Matthias cf.: E. Haraszti, "Pierre Bono — Luthiste de Mathia Corvin", *RdM* XXVIII (1949), 73 ff.; O. Gombosi, "Vita musicale . . .", 110 ff.; G. Reese, *Music in the Renaissance*, 717-23; L. Fokövi, "Musik und Musikalische Verhältnisse in Ungarn am Hofe von Matthias Corvinus", *Kirchenmusikalisches Jahrbuch* XV (1900), 1 ff.; *New Oxford History of Music*, III, 301 f.; B. Szabolcsi, *Geschichte der Ungarischen Musik*, Budapest (1964), 19-22. For the general cultural environment see Berzeviczy, *op. cit.*, I, 240-67.

directed by Johannes Stokhem, was superior to the Papal choir, whereupon, at least to quote Haberl, the Pope ordered his choir to be enlarged to 24 singers [88].

The time of Matthias' reign was for Hungary a time of security and of glorious conquests. He succeeded in keeping the Turks off his border and in penetrating into Bosnia. In 1485 he conquered Vienna and his reputation grew as he gradually became the representative of the mightiest power of Central Europe. Culturally too the court of Buda ambitiously tried to emulate the example of the North Italian courts. King Matthias was a great bibliophile and supplied his *Corvina* library with expensive, splendidly illuminated parchment manuscripts, including music codices [89]. He invited artists such as Vassari and Francesco Cellini to Buda and charged them with special commissions.

Through the marriage of Matthias and Beatrice cultural life at the court of Buda was intensified. New family ties associated it with the courts of Naples, Ferrara (Leonora, sister of Beatrice, was the wife of Ercole d'Este of Ferrara), Mantua (Isabella, the wife of Francesco of Gonzaga, was a niece of Beatrice) and Milano (Beatrice, wife of Ludovico de More, was another niece of hers). Beatrice's correspondence bears witness to close musical relations with these courts. Singers, instrumentalists and composers were sent to Buda at her request, amongst whom we should mention the lutenist Pietro Bono, the singer Jean Cornuel and the composers Johann Stokhem, Erasmus Lampicida and Jacobus Barbireau (the latter probably came on a political mission for Maximilian I) [90].

The music played at the Hungarian court displayed, according to Haraszti [91], Franco-Flemish influences in its vocal style and German elements, transmitted through Italy, in its instrumental style. Burgundian culture and music which spread all over fifteenth century Europe reached Hungary, too. On the political level Matthias had negotiations with Charles the Bold about a combat against the common Turkish enemy. As belonging

88 Cf. E. Haraszti, *op. cit.*, 75.

89 Among them, for instance, was a liturgical MS, Codex 41 a, with illuminated initials showing the Hungarian Court Choir, numbering eleven singers. Cf. I. Mészaros, "The Choir of King Matthias, illustrated in a Corvina Manuscript", *Muszica*, Budapest (Dec. 1962), 36-37 (in Hungarian).

90 Cf. O. Gombosi, "Jacobus Barbireaus letzte Lebensjahre", *ZfMw* XII (1930), 378 and Reese, *op. cit.*, 723.

91 "Pierre Bono . . .", *RdM* XXVIII, 73.

to the musicians of the Hungarian court meant recommendation everywhere, Maximilian I took some musicians from the court of Matthias with him on one of his journeys, and after Matthias' death he employed many of his musicians at his court [92].

This outline of musical conditions at the courts of Naples and Buda should suffice to explain many of the statements of the anonymous author of the epigram, which so clearly stresses the rôle of Beatrice as a patron of culture. Obscure as this dedication appears to be, some conclusions may nevertheless be drawn from it:

1) Beatrice is addressed as *Ungarie Regina.* Accordingly they could have been dedicated to her only after her betrothal to Matthias Corvinus in 1475. For immediately after her betrothal (i.e. already before the marriage) Beatrice was addressed with her new regal title, as proved, for example, by the accounts of the Neapolitan court for that year [93].

2) The epigram (line 9 to end) indicates that Matthias is still alive. Thus it cannot have been written after 1490, the year of his death. We may therefore conclude that the *terminus a quo* for the dedication of the manuscript is 1475, while the *terminus ante quem* for the origin of the Masses would be 1490.

3) In line 15 a certain *Charolus princeps* occurs, to whom the Masses were known before. From the construction of the sentence it is obvious that the comparison (*Charolus hoc . . . gaudere solebat / conveniet . . . moribus . . . tuis*) refers to a high personality, who by virtue of his rank may have been close to the Queen. The title, *princeps*, however, clearly distinguishes between *princeps* and *rex*. It seems clear that by *Charolus princeps* none other than Charles the Bold, Duke of Burgundy, is meant.

Charles the Bold had maintained political relations with Ferrante as early as in 1471, being allied with him against their common Turkish and French enemies [94]. In 1474 a plan was hatched to betrothe his daughter Maria (who was later to marry Maximilian I) to the second son of Ferrante [95]. In 1475 Charles visited Naples [96], an occasion which was certainly marked by great ceremonies and musical festivities. Charles the Bold him-

92 *Ibid.*

93 Berzeviczy, *op. cit.*, 95 ff.

94 E. Dürr, "Karl der Kühne und der Ursprung des Habsburg-Spanischen Imperiums", *Historische Zeitschrift*, (1914), 95 ff.

95 Berzeviczy, *ibid.*, 98.

96 Cf. article "Neapel", *MGG* IX.

self was an ardent music lover, and at his court musicians such as Busnois, Morton and Hayne van Ghizeghem were engaged. In 1460, for instance, he visited Cambrai, where the choristers of the chapel performed in his presence a motet, which he had himself composed [97]. As it is known that the Burgundian dukes often used to take their court musicians with them on their journeys, it is very likely that Charles and his musicians, while on their visit to Naples, got to know the rich musical life of that town, and possibly even the musical skill of Beatrice. Later, political relations between Burgundy and Hungary became even closer, for Charles lost his confidence in his former ally Georg Podiebrat, King of Bohemia, and drew nearer to Matthias, mainly on account of their common enemy, the Turk [98].

After the death of Charles the Bold in 1477 his court musicians passed to his daughter Maria, and one year later to her husband, Maximilian I of Habsburg. It may be assumed that after Charles' death a musician of the Burgundian court in search of a new employer sought, through the dedication of the manuscript, to gain favour with the Hungarian Queen, whose musical talents he had often heard praised, or even might have witnessed himself during his Neapolitan sojourn.

The above conclusion casts new light on the circumstances in which the composition originated: The Masses could have been already composed *before* 1475, and may not have been intended *a priori* for the Queen, but may have originated at the Burgundian court and known — at least as stated in the epigram — to Charles the Bold.

The assumption, that the *L'Homme armé* Masses belong to the Burgundian-Flemish circle of Dufay and Busnois and not to the Neapolitan circle of Tinctoris — as has often been claimed [99] — is reinforced by two further indications: Firstly, the Gothic writing, the longish shape of the notes, the style of the blazon and the French motto — all speak against the possibility of Italian provenance. Secondly, lines 3-6 of the dedication, taken literally, appear to give us exact information. The Queen's virtues are proclaimed all over the world, and reach even *nostris locis*. It follows, therefore, that the composer could not possibly be a compatriot of Queen Beatrice but must be an inhabitant of another, distant country. Likewise the description of the Queen who brings culture and music with her to the

97 Cf. A Pirro, *Histoire . . .*, 115 ff.

98 M. Brion, *Charles le Téméraire*, Paris (1947), 159 ff.

99 Cf., for instance, Reese, *op. cit.*, 150.

new, far-off country (*regionibus istis*, and not *regionibus his*), indicates — if one may take them literally — that the composer could not be a Hungarian.

We have tried to draw the limits of time and place, within which we suppose the Masses to have been composed, but nothing has as yet been said about the author and the actual origin of the composition. As we return to the stylistic analysis of the composition the problems described before again arise, i.e. the archaic aspect of these Masses, the monumentality of the structure, the peculiar co-existence of progressive and retrospective tendencies. The stylistic discrepancies which may be observed between the six Masses — e.g. the relatively advanced texture of the second, and in part also of the third Mass, the antiquated style of the sixth, the "Dufayisms" of the first Mass — all these provide perhaps the key to the riddle: were the six Masses indeed composed by one composer? The evidence that, except for the common plan ruling all six Masses, no further thematic reference exists between them, together with the unusually large dimensions of the composition, points to the explanation that several composers collaborated in the project. One is reminded of the kind of workshop collaboration well known in the plastic arts. The original structure of the whole may have been laid down in outline by the "Master", the realization being distributed amongst his pupils. This would explain the otherwise inexplicable differences of stylistic and technical approach encountered in the six Masses. These appear to stem from divergencies between the individual styles of a number of composers, who are nevertheless using the same musical language and idiom.

The most famous musician of the Burgundian Court at the time of Charles the Bold was Antoine Busnois, who had already been in Charles' service during the life time of this father, Philip the Good, and who used to accompany Charles between 1471-1477 on his journeys and campaigns. After 1477 his name often appears in accounts of Maria of Burgundy and her husband Maximilian I. Busnois, mainly a composer of chansons, enjoyed great reputation during his life and even after his death (about 1492). He was praised by his contemporaries Molinet, Ramis de Pareja, Hothby, Compère and Tinctoris. In Venice his works were still being performed posthumously in 1495, and as late as 1545 his name was mentioned in Pietro Aron's *Toscanello in Musica* [100]. Like the designer of these Masses

100 Cf. article "Busnois", *MGG* II.

and, indeed, like his other contemporaries, Busnois also took great pleasure in poetical allusions and musical contrivances. In his Mass *Anthoni usque limina*, for example, he seems to enjoy the word play *Anthoni usque* [101]; in the motet *In hydraulis* [102] a three note motif is used and repeated over and over again in transposition of the fourth and the fifth. His tenors, including the tenor of his famous *L'Homme armé* Mass are expanded according to strict rythmical schemes. In his treatment of canons and of imitations, too, Busnois recalls in many details the composer (or composers) of the Neapolitan Masses, although his writing is more advanced in technique. In his own *L'Homme armé* Mass, for example, the alto participates in canonical episodes; in the *Gloria* the motif of the descending fifth (motif b′, cf. example 1) pervades all the voices (at *tu solus altissimus*); at the beginning of each movement the alto anticipates the head motif of the c.f., and the *Osanna* is set only once (as in Masses 2, 4, 5 and 6 of the cycle). The Mass is based on a version of the *L'Homme armé* chanson, which is identical with that of the Neapolitan Masses.

Despite the more advanced technique of Busnois' writing — at least in his Masses and chansons — melodically many similarities exist between his compositions and the Neapolitan Masses. Especially in those sections of our Masses written in *tempus imperfectum* we find motifs reminiscent of the Burgundian chansonesque style of Busnois. One should compare for instance the motto of the *Crucifixus* of Mass 2, which is repeated several times, with the beginning of Busnois' *Cent Mille escus* [103]:

ex. 29

If we consider all this: Busnois' pleasure in musical and literary devices, his musical style and technique, the fact that in his known *L'Homme armé* Mass he uses exactly the same version of the song that also appears in the

[101] Cf. Reese, *ibid.*, 109; E. Sparks, Cantus firmus in Mass and *Motet, 1420-1520*, Berkeley (1963), 212-18.

[102] *Denkmäler der Tonkunst in Oesterreich*, VII, 105.

[103] *EDM*, IV, 67.

Neapolitan Masses (cf. p. 23) and above all his rôle at the court of *Charolus princeps*, it gradually becomes evident that the idea of the Mass cycle originated within Busnois' circle at the Burgundian court.

Busnois' famous *L'Homme armé* Mass, which enjoyed great reputation up to the first half of the sixteenth century (cf. above, note 22), was composed — as supposes O. Strunk (*ibid.*) — around 1475, and R. Hannas even tries to point to the historical circumstances of its composition: "We may hazard a guess that it [i.e. Busnois' *L'Homme armé* Mass] belongs in the year 1475, at which Busnois' patron, Charles the Bold, attempted final negotiations with the cascillating Frederick III" [104].

The exact date of the notorious meeting between Frederick III and Charles the Bold at Trèves was September 20, 1473. It could be very plausible to assume that Busnois, Charles' court composer, had composed a Mass especially for this event, and even to "hazard a guess" that the whole cycle of the *L'Homme armé* Masses was composed to serve as musical embellishment of the solemn Masses, to be celebrated during the weeks of the meeting. Unfortunately, we have to discard this theory, which is not supported by any evidence. On the contrary, it seems that the Neapolitan Masses do not stem from the years around 1473, for they demonstrate a technique less advanced than, for instance, Busnois' *L'Homme armé* Mass described before. As far as it is at all possible to determine the exact date of a composition within a time span of five years, it seems that the Masses were composed between 1465 and 1470 [105]. It is also possible that the cycle was not commissioned for any specific political event but was composed as an experiment, speculating on problems of structure and playing with the famous tune and with the associations it carries with it.

Many questions as yet remain unanswered: Did Busnois, the "Master" himself, take part in the team work, or did he confine himself to the task of planning and instructing? Did he himself, perhaps, compose the second Mass, the style of which is reminiscent of his musical language? What is the reason for the "Dufayisms" of the first Mass? Who were the composers who cooperated in the composition of the cycle? Similarly, we do not yet

104 *JAMS* V (1952), 168. In *JAMS* VI (1953), 93, R. Hannas erroneously corrects the date to 1478.

105 Cf. also O. Gombosi, "Vita musicale . . .", 128, who assumed on stylistic grounds that the Masses were composed at the end of the sixth decade of the fifteenth century, "forse intorno 1470". On the other hand, his statement that the Masses show many similarities with the style of Ockeghem is not demonstrated.

know the identity of the composer who had participated in the composition, and who presented the manuscript to Beatrice after Charles' death. Anyhow, Beatrice seems to have taken that *munus ab ignoto* into her personal possession and to have brought the manuscript back with her in 1501 to Naples where it has apparently remained to this day.

Undoubtedly Charles the Bold really "found pleasure" in this composition. Indeed, his interest in it was perhaps not purely a musical one. For the political connotations of the *L'Homme armé* song, which so obviously dominates the whole composition, must have struck the last Burgundian duke, Charles the Bold, in whose mind "sein politischer Lebenszweck nur diese bildhaften Formen angenommen hat: der Ruhm Alexanders und Hannibals, die Ehre seines Geschlechts in der Rache gegen Ludwig XI, das Herrschaftsideal, nicht mehr Lehnfürst zu sein, das heilige Ritterideal Jerusalem" [106], saw as the goal of his life the fight against and final victory over the *doubté turcq*. This idea of a crusade he inherited from his father, whom Pope Pius II (Aeneas Sylvius) had chosen as late as 1463 to be one of the leaders of the crusade then planned [107]. In all the contracts signed between Charles and the Powers of the Mediterranean area, such as Venice, Naples and Aragon, the common fight against the Turk is mentioned. And as told by Olivier de la Marche in his *Mémoires*, "his wish and his passion was to go to war himself against the infidel, and he wanted to be so big and powerful, as to become leader of other peoples, for he did not want to be subject to anybody" [108].

Only within this political and spiritual situation can the creation of this monumental composition be explained, where secular ideas of arms and war are clad in liturgical trappings, and in which the tenor is not only a *fundamentum totius relationis* in the accepted musical and technical meaning, but serves as a point of departure and a spiritual stimulus throughout the whole composition. It is, indeed, this fusion of the secular and the sacred which is so highly characteristical of "The Waning of the Middle Ages".

106 J. Huizinga, "Burgund — eine Krise des Romanisch Germanischen Verhältnisses", *Im Bann der Geschichte*, Basel (1943), 319.

107 Cf. A. S. Atiya, *The Crusade in the Later Middle Ages*, New York (1965[2]), 229.

108 German text in E. Dürr, "Karl der Kühne . . .", 52 f.

APPENDIX: LIST OF *L'HOMME ARMÉ* COMPOSITIONS

The following list does not claim to be comprehensive. Several items, however, were added here to earlier lists made by O. Gombosi (*Jacob Obrecht,* 1925, 47) and G. Reese (*Music in the Renaissance,* 1954, 992). A list of *L'Homme armé* chansons and instrumental pieces has not been published before.

In the following, only modern editions, not original sources are listed. Partial editions have not been noted when a complete edition of the same composition exists. Only if no edition at all has appeared, sources (in the first place printed) and partial editions were registered.

A. MASSES

I. Complete Masses

Basiron: *MPLSER,* no. 8.

Brumel: *Anton Brumel, Opera Omnia* I, *CMM* 5, Rome 1951 (ed. by A. Carapetyan)

Busnois: MPLSER, no. 2.

Carissimi: Rome, MS *Capp. Lat.*

Caron: *MPLSER,* no. 3.

Carver: *Musica Britannica* XV, London 1957 (ed. by K. Elliott).

Compère: *Loyset Compère, Opera Omnia* I, Rome 1958 (ed. by L. Finscher).

Dufay: 1. *Dufay* O III, part 2, 1951; 2. *MPLSER,* no. 1.

Faugues: *MPLSER,* no. 4.

Forestier: Rome, MS *Capp. Sist.,* 160 (under the name "Mathurin Forestyn").

Josquin: Mass I: *Super voces musicales, Josquin MS* I, 1931. — Mass II: *Sexti toni, Josquin MS* I, 1931. — Mass III: *L'ome armé* in MS. Munich, *Bayr. Staatsbibliothek,* MS Mus 3154, and Leipzig, *Bibl. der Thomaskirche,* MS 51. Smijers attributed this Mass to Compère. (Cf. M. Antonowytsch, "The Present State of Josquin Research", *International Musicological Society. Congress Report,* New York, 1961, 58.)

La Rue: Mass I. Four part Mass.: 1. *Misse Petri de La Rue,* Venice 1503 (publ. by O. Petrucci); 2. *Kyrie* and *Et incarnatus* in O. Gombosi, *Jacob Obrecht,* 36 and 39; 3. *Kyrie* I and II in A. T. Davison and W. Apel, *Historical Anthology of Music* I, Cambridge, Mass., 1946, 95. — Mass II. Four parts ex three: 1. Rome, MS *Capp. Sist.* 34; 2. Jena, *Universitätsbibliothek,* MS 2; 3. *Kyrie* I in E. Roediger, *Die geistlichen Musikhandschriften der Universitätsbibliothek Jena,* Jena 1935, *Notenverzeichnis,* 1.

Morales: Mass I. Five part Mass.: *Cristobal de Morales, Opera Omnia, Monumentos de la Música Española* XI, Rome 1952 (ed. by H. Anglés). — Mass II. Four part

Mass.: 1. *Christophori Moralis Hyspalensis missarum liber* II, Lyon 1544 (publ. by V. and L Dorico); 2. *Christophori Moralis Hyspalensis missarum liber* II, Lyon 1551 (publ. by J. Moderne).

Mouton: 1. MS Jena, *Universitätsbibliothek*; 2. *Kyrie* I in Roediger, *op. cit.*, *Notenverzeichnis*, 6.

Obrecht: *Jakob Obrecht, Werken* V, Leipzig 1908-21 (ed. by J. Wolf).

Ockeghem: 1. *Ockeghem W* I, 1927; 2. *MPLSER*, no. 6.

de Orto: *MPLSER*, no. 7.

Palestrina: Mass I. Five part Mass.: 1. *Giovanni Pierluigi da Palestrinas Werke* XII, Leipzig 1862-1907 (ed. by F. X. Haberl); 2. *Giovanni Pierluigi da Palestrina, Le Opere Complete* VI, Rome 1939 (ed. by R. Casimiri). — Mass II. Four part Mass.: 1. *Werke* XIII; 2. Opere X, 1940.

Peñalosa: MS Tarazona, *Catedral, Archivio Musical*, 2. (Cf. H. Anglés, *Monumentos* . . . I, 124).

Pipelare: *Matthaeus Pipelare Opera Omnia* III, *CMM* 34, Rome 1967 (ed. by R. Cross).

Regis: 1. *Opera Omnia Johannis Regis* I, *CMM* 9, Rome 1956 (ed. by C. W. H. Lindenburg); 2. *MPLSER*, no. 5.

Senfl: *Ludwig Senfl, Sämtliche Werke* I, *EDM* 5, Leipzig 1937 (ed. by E. Löhrer and O. Ursprung).

Tinctoris: *MPLSER*, no. 9.

Vacqeras: *MPLSER*, no. 10.

II. Uncertain authorship and anonymous compositions

Anonymous: Six Masses in Naples, *Bibl. Naz.*, MS VI E 40 (for edition see note 2).

— *Missa Le om'armé* in Barcelona. MS *Bibl. Central*, 454. (Cf. H. Anglés, *Monumentos* . . . I, 112).

Guerrero(?): *L'Homme armé* Mass in Avila, *Real Monasterio de santa Ana*. (Cf. *Grove's Dictionary of Music and Musicians* II, 3rd edition, New York 1952, 477; but cf. also R. Stevenson, *Spanish Cathedral Music in the Golden Age*, Berkeley 1961, 187).

Ortiz(?): a *L'Homme armé* Mass by him mentioned in *Un tratedo de Canto de Organo* (attributed to Vincente Lusitano). Diego or Miguel Ortiz may be meant. (Cf. R. Stevenson, *ibid.*, 322).

III. Single Mass movements and fragments

Juan de Anchieta: *Missa quarti toni*; *Agnus* based on the c.f. *L'Homme armé*. Tarazona, MS 3. (Cf. R. Stevenson, *Spanish Music in the Age of Columbus*, Berkeley 1960, 137 and 153; H. Anglés, *Monumentos* . . . I, 1-34, *parte musicale*).

Anonymous: *Agnus L'Homme armé*, *cantus* and tenor, bass presumably lacking. (Cf. K. Elliott, "The Carver Choir-Book", *Music and Letters* XLI (1960), 349 ff.

Costanzo Festa: *Missa diversorum tenorum. Kyrie* based in the c.f. *L'Homme armé. (Italia Sacra Musica* III, Copenhagen 1962, ed. by K. Jeppesen).

Vitalis Venedier: *Missa L'Homme armé,* alto and bass preserved in part books. Berlin, Bibliothek Werner Wolffheim. (Cf. *Ockeghem W,* I, ii).

B. SECULAR COMPOSITIONS

I. Chansons

Anonymous: Four part chanson. (Cf. Obrecht, *Werken* V, 95).

Josquin: Four part chanson. (Cf. *Van Ockeghem tot Sweelinck,* Amsterdam 1939, 155, ed. by A. Smijers).

Morton: Four part chanson. (Cf. J. Marix, *Les Musiciens de la Cour de Bourgogne au XVe siècle,* Paris 1939, 86; 2. V. Lederer, *Ueber Heimat und Ursprung der mehrstimmigen Tonkunst,* Leipzig 1906, 425 (with errors); 3. J. Obrecht, *Werken* V, 94 (author named "Borton").

II. Double chansons

Anonymous: The version of the *Mellon Chansonnier,* in three parts, the *L'Homme armé* melody contained in the tenor. (Cf. M. Bukofzer, "An Unknown Chansonnier of the 15th Century", *MQ* XXVIII (1942), 14 ff.

Basiron: Four part song, the *L'Homme armé* melody contained in the tenor and *D'ung autre amer* (by Ockeghem) in the *cantus.* (*Van Ockeghem . . .,* 30).

Japart: Four part song, containing the *L'Homme armé* melody in the bass and *Il est de bonne heure né* in *cantus* and tenor. (Cf. H. M. Brown, *Theatrical Chansons of the 15th and early 16th Century,* Cambridge, Mass., 1963, 79).

III. Quodlibets

Tinctoris: In his *Proportionale,* chap. IV, there appears a quodlibet combining O *Rosa bella* (*cantus*), *L'Homme armé* (tenor; beginning only), *Et robinet* (bass). (Cf. Couss. IV, 173).

IV. Instrumental pieces

Branle L'Homme armé in *The Dublin Virginal Manuscript, The Wellesley edition* III, Wellesley, Mass. 1954, 22 (ed. by J. M. Ward). For a *contrafactum* of the *cantus* of this branle see *ibid.,* 51.

On p. 51 of Ward's edition the following *L'Homme armé* branles are mentioned:

Sebastian Vreedman: *L'Homme armé* in *Liber secundus,* fol. 16'.

Fruytiers, *Ecclesiasticus* (ed. by D. F. Scheurleer, Amsterdam 1898, 95).

Thysius, *Luitboek,* once with the text *Compt ghy gesellekens coene* and once as *Branle.* (Ed. by J. P. N. Land, *Het Luitboek van Thysius,* Amsterdam 1889, 36 and 111).

In 1930 Johann Nepomuk David composed a *Phantasia super L'Homme armé,* for organ.

BIBLIOGRAPHY

Adler, G., *Handbuch der Musikgeschichte* I, Frankfurt 1929.

Ambros, A. W., *Geschichte der Musik*, Vol. III, Leipzig 1868; Vol. V, Breslau 1911 (ed. by O. Kade).

Antonowytsch, M., "The present State of Josquin Research", *International Musicological Society. Congress Report*, New York 1961, 58.

Apel, W., "Imitation Canons on *L'Homme armé*", *Speculum* XXV (1950), 367.

— *Die Notation der polyphonen Musik*, Leipzig 1962.

Apfel, E.: "Zur Entstehung des Palestrina Satzes", *AfMw* IV (1957), 30.

Atiya, A. S., *The Crusade in the Later Middle-Ages*, New York 1965².

Berzeviczy, A. de, *Béatrice d'Aragon, Reine d'Hongrie*, Paris 1911.

Besseler, H., *Bourdon und Fauxbourdon*, Leipzig 1950.

— "Die Entstehung der Posaune", *Acta* XXII (1950), 8.

— *Musik des Mittelalters und der Renaissance*, Potsdam 1931.

— "Neue Dokumente zum Leben und Schaffen Dufays", *AfMw* IX (1952), 156.

— "Von Dufay bis Josquin", *ZfMw* XI (1928), 1.

Van den Borren, C., *Etudes sur le XVe siècle musical*, Antwerpen 1941.

— "Quelques réflexions à própos du style imitatif synatxique", *Revue Belge de Musicoilogie* I (1946), 14.

Brion, M., *Charles le Témeraire, Grand duc d'Occident*, Paris 1947.

Brooks, C., "Antoine Busnois, Chanson Composer", *JAMS VI* (1953), 111.

Brown, H. M., "The Chanson rustique: Popular Elements in the 15th and 16th-Century Chanson", *JAMS* XII, (1959), 16.

— *Theatrical Chansons of the 15th and early 16th Century*, Cambridge, Mass. 1963.

Brumel, A., *Antoine Brumel, Opera Omnia I, CMM* 5, Rome 1951 (ed. by A. Carapetyan).

Bukofzer, M., "An Unknown Chansonnier of the 15th Century", *MQ* XXVIII (1942), 14.

— *Studies in Medieval and Renaissance Music*, London, 1950.

Calmette, J., *The Golden Age of Burgundy, the magnificent Dukes and their Courts*, London, 1962.

The Cambridge Medieval History VIII, Cambridge 1936.

Carver, R., *Missa L'Homme armé*, in *Musica Britannica* XV, London 1957 (ed. by K. Elliott).

Compère, L., *Loyset Compère, Opera Omnia* I, *CMM* 15, Rome 1958 (ed. by L. Finscher).

Davison, A. T. and W. Apel, *Historical Anthology of Music* I, Cambridge, Mass., 1949.

Dent, E., "William Byrd and the Madrigal", *Festschrift Johannes Wolf*, Berlin 1929.

Dürr, E., "Karl der Kühne und der Ursprung des Habsburgisch-Spanischen Imperiums", *Historische Zeitschrift* CXIII (1914).

Dufay, G., *Guglielmi Dufay Opera Omnia*, Rome 1948- (ed. by H. Besseler and G. de Van).

Eitner, R., *Biographisch-bibliographisches Quellenlexikon der Musiker und Musikgelehrten*, 2. edition Graz 1959-60.

Elliott, K., "The Carver Choir-Book", *Music and Letters* XLI (1960), 349.

Enciclopedia Italiana, Milan 1931-39.

Feininger, L., *Die Frühgeschichte des Kanons*, diss. Heidelberg 1937.

Feldmann, F., "Untersuchungen zum Wort-Ton Verhältnis in den Gloria und Credosätzen von Dufay bis Josquin", *MD* VIII (1954), 141.

Fokövi, L., "Musik und musikalische Verhältnisse in Ungarn am Hofe von Matthias Corvinus", *Kirchenmusikalisches Jahrbuch* XV (1900), 1.

Fulda, A. von, *Musica*, in Gerbert, M. (ed.), *Scriptores ecclesiastici de musica* III, facsim. edition Milan 1931, 329.

Gafurio, F., *Practica musicae*, Milan 1496.

Georgiades, T., *Musik und Sprache: Das Werden der abendländischen Musik, dargestellt an der Vertonung der Messe*, Berlin 1954.

Glareanus, H., *Dodecachordon*, Basel 1547. German by F. Bohn, Leipzig 1888.

Gombosi, O., "Die ältesten Denkmäler der mehrstimmigen Vokalmusik aus Ungarn", *Ungarische Jahrbücher* IX (1931), 84.
— "Bemerkungen zur *L'Homme armé* Frage, *ZfMw* X (1928), 609.
— "Gothic Form", *MD* IV (1950), 43.
— *Jacob Obrecht, eine Stilkritische Studie*, Berlin 1935.
— "Jacobus Barbireaus letzte Lebensjahre", *ZfMw* XII (1930), 378.
— "Vita musicale alle Corte di Re Mattia", *Corvina* XII (1929), 110.

Grove's Dictionary of Music and Musicians, 3rd. edition, New York 1928: article "Guerrero"; 5th edition, New York 1954: articles "Carver", "Guerrero", "Mass".

Handschin, J., *Musikgeschichte im Ueberblick*, Luzern 1948.

Hannas, R., "Concerning deletions in the Polyphonic Mass Credo", *JAMS* V (1952), 155.

Haraszti, E., "Les Musiciens de Mathias Corvin et de Béatrice d'Aragon", *La Musique instrumentale de la Renaissance*, Paris 1955, 35.
— "Pierre Bono, Luthiste de Mathias Corvin", *RdM* I (1949), 73.

Harrison, F. L., "The Eton Choirbook, its Background and Contents", *Annales Musicologiques* I (1953), 151.

Hermelink, S., *Dispositionis modorum*, in *Münchener Veröffentlichungen zur Musikgeschichte* IV, Munich 1960.

Huizinga, J., *Herbst des Mittelalters*, Munich 1929.

— *Im Bann der Geschichte*, Basle 1943.

Italia Sacra Musica III, Copenhagen 1962 (ed. by K. Jeppesen).

Jeppesen, K., *Counterpoint*, New York 1939.

Josquin des Prés, *Missen* I, Amsterdam-Leipzig 1931 (ed. by A. Smijers).

Krenek, E., *Johannes Ockeghem*, New York 1953.

Lach, R., *Studien zur Entwicklungsgeschichte der ornamentalen Melopöie*, diss. Vienna 1902.

Lang, P. H., *Music in Western Civilization*, New York 1941.

Lederer, V., *Ueber Heimat und Ursprung der mehrstimmigen Tonkunst*, Leipzig 1906.

Lowinsky, E., *Tonality and Atonality in 16th Century Music*, Berkeley 1961.

Machaut, G. de, *Messe Nôtre Dame*, in *Polyphonic Music of the Fourteenth Century* III, Monaco 1956 (ed. by L. Schrade).

Mancusi, E., "Il liber Coralis notis musicis ornatus, MS VI E 40", *Il Rievocatore* XII (1961), no. 1-3.

Marix, J., *Histoire de la musique et de musiciens de la cour de Bourgogne sous le règne de Philippe le Bon*, Strasburg 1939.

— *Les Musiciens de la cour de Bourgogne au XVe siècle (1420-1467)*, Paris 1937.

Meier, B., "Caput, Bemerkungen zur Messe Dufays und Ockeghems", *Mf* VII (1954), 268.

— "Die Hs. Porto 714 als Quelle zur Tonartenlehre des 15. Jahrhunderts", *MD* VII (1953), 175.

— "Die Harmonik im c.f.-haltigen Satz des 15. Jahrhunderts", *AfMw* IX (1952), 27.

— "Zyklische Gesamtstruktur und Tonalität in den Messen Jacob Obrechts", *AfMw* X (1953), 289.

Mészaros, I., "The Choir of King Matthias, illustrated in a Corvina Manuscript", *Muszica*, Dec. 1962, 36-37. (In Hungarian).

Monumenta Polyphoniae Liturgicae Sanctae Ecclesiae Romanae, ser. I, Rome 1948 (ed. by L. Feininger). Contains 10 L'Homme armé Masses by Dufay, Busnois, Caron, Faugues, Regis, Ockeghem, de Orto, Basiron, Tinctoris and Vacqueras.

Monumentos de la Música Española (ed. by H. Anglés). Vol. I, Rome 1941; Vol. XI, Rome 1952.

Morales, C. de, *Missa L'Homme armé a 5 vocis*, in *Cristóbal de Morales, Opera Omnia. Monumentos* . . . XI, Rome 1952 (ed. by H. Anglés).

Die Musik in Geschichte und Gegenwart, Kassel 1949-. Articles "Busnois", "Color", "Dufay", "Dunstable", "Messe", "Neapel", "Obrecht", "Ockeghem" and others.

New Oxford History of Music III, London 1960.

Obrecht, J., *Jakob Obrecht, Werken*, Leipzig 1908-21 (ed. by J. Wolf).

Ockeghem, J., *Johannes Ockeghem, Sämtliche Werke*, Leipzig 1927 and 1947 (ed. by D. Plamenac).

Palestrina, G. P. da, *Giovanni Pierluigi da Palestrina, Le Opere Complete* (ed. by R. Casimiri). Vol. VI, Rome 1939. Vol. X, Rome 1940.

Pipelare, M., *Missa L'Homme armé*, in *Matthaeus Pipelare Opera Omnia* III, *CMM* 34, Rome 1967 (ed. by R. Cross).

Pirenne, H., *Histoire de Belgique* II, Brussels 1922.

Pirro, A., *Histoire de la musique de la fin du XIVe siècle à la fin du XVIe*, Paris 1940,

Plamenac, D., "Antwort zu Gombosi", *ZfMw* XI (1929), 376.

— "La Chanson de *L'Homme armé* et le manuscrit VI E 40 de la Bibliothèque nationale de Naples", *Annales de la Fédération archéologique et historique de Belgique, Congrès jubilaire*, 1925, 229.

Polyphonia Sacra, London 1932 (ed. by C. Van den Borren).

Pope, I., "La Musique Espagnole à la cour de Naples dans la seconde moitiée du XVe siècle", *Musique et Poésie au XVIe siècle*, Paris 1954.

Power, L., *Missa super Alma Redemptoris Mater*, in *Documenta Polyphoniae Liturgicae Sanctae Ecclesiae Romanae*, ser. I, Rome 1947 (ed. by L. Feininger).

Reese, G., *Music in the Renaissance*, New York 1954.

Regis, J., *Opera Omnia Johannis Regis* I, *CMM* 9, Rome 1956 (ed. by C. W. H. Lindenburg).

Reichert, G., "Kirchentonart als Formfaktor in der mehrstimmigen Musik des 15. und 16. Jahrhunderts", *Mf* IV (1951), 35.

Roediger, E., *Die geistlichen Musikhandschriften der Universitätsbibliothek Jena*, Jena 1935.

Saar, J. du, *Jacobus Barbireau*, Utrecht 1946.

Sachs, C., *Reallexikon der Musikinstrumente*, Berlin 1913.

— *The History of Musical Instruments*, New York 1950.

Schrade, L., "Renaissance: The Historical Concept of an Epoch", *Kongressbericht Utrecht* 1952, 19.

Senfl, L., *Ludwig Senfl, Sämtliche Werke* I, *EDM* 5, Leipzig 1937 (ed. by E. Löhrer and O. Ursprung).

Sparks, E. H., *Cantus firmus in Mass and Motet, 1420-1520*, Berkeley 1963.

Stephan, W., *Die Burgundisch-Niederländische Motette zur Zeit Ockeghems*, Kassel 1937.

Stevenson, R., *Spanish Cathedral Music in the Golden Age*, Berkeley 1961.

— *Spanish Music in the Age of Columbus*, Berkely 1960.

Straeten, E. van der, *La Musique aux Pays Bas*, Brussels 1867-88.

Strunk, O., "The Origins of the *L'Homme armé* Mass, *BAMS* 1936, 25.

— Review of the edition of Leonel Power, *Missa super Alma Redemptoris Mater*, *JAMS* II (1949), 107.

Szabolcsi, B., *Geschichte der Ungarischen Musik*, Budapest 1964.

Tinctoris, J., *Proportionale, Liber de arte contrapuncti, Liber de natura et proprietate tonorum, Diffinitorium musicae*, in E. de Coussemaker, *Scriptorum de Musica*

Medii Aevi IV, Paris 1864-76.

Ursprung, O., *Katholische Kirchenmusik*, Potsdam 1931.

Van Ockeghem tot Sweelinck, Amsterdam 1939-56 (ed. by A. Smijers).

Wagner, P., *Geschichte der Messe* I, Leipzig 1913.

Ward, J. (ed.), *The Dublin Virginal Manuscript*, in *The Wellesley Editions* III, Wellesley, Mass. 1954.

Wienpahl, R., "Modal Usages in Masses of the Fifteenth Century", *JAMS* V (1952), 37.

Wolff, H., *Die Musik der alten Niederländer*, Leipzig 1950.

— "Die Variationstechnik in den frühen Messen Palestrinas", *Acta* XXVII (1957), 59.

Zarlino, G., *Istituzioni harmoniche*, edition Venice 1562.

Zenck, H., "Zarlinos *Istitutioni harmoniche* als Quelle zur Musikanschauung der italienischen Renaissance", *ZfMw* XII (1929-30), 540.

ABBREVIATIONS

Acta	Acta Musicologica
AfMw	Archiv für Musikwissenschaft
BAMS	Bulletins of the American Musicological Society
CMM	Corpus Mensurabilis Musicae
Couss.	C. E. de Coussemaker (ed.), Scriptorum de Musica Medii Aevi. Paris 1864-76
Dufay O	Guglielmi Dufay Opera Omnia, *CMM* 1, Rome 1948- (ed. by H. Besseler and G. de Van)
EDM	Das Erbe Deutscher Musik
JAMS	Journal of the American Musicological Society
Josquin MS	Josquin des Prês, Missen. Amsterdam-Leipzig 1931- (ed. by A. A. Smijers)
MD	Musica Disciplina
Mf	Die Musikforschung
MGG	Die Musik in Geschichte und Gegenwart
MPLSER	Monumenta Polyphoniae Liturgicae Sanctae Ecclesiae Romanae, series I, vol. i, Rome 1948 (ed. by L. Feininger)
MQ	The Musical Quarterly
Ockeghem W	Johannes Ockeghem, Sämtliche Werke. Leipzig 1927- (ed. by D. Plamenac)
RdM	Revue de Musicologie
ZfMw	Zeitschrift für Musikwissenschaft